BREAKOUT

BREAKOUT

Profiles in
African
Rhythm

GARY STEWART

The University of Chicago Press • Chicago and London

A freelance critic of African music, Gary Stewart has published pieces in
The Beat, West Africa, and *Reggae and African Beat.*

The University of Chicago Press, Chicago 60637
The University of Chicago Press, Ltd., London
© 1992 by The University of Chicago
All rights reserved. Published 1992
Printed in the United States of America
01 00 99 98 97 96 95 94 93 92   5 4 3 2 1

ISBN (cloth): 0-226-77405-8
ISBN (paper): 0-226-77406-6

Library of Congress Cataloging-in-Publication Data
Stewart, Gary.
    Breakout : profiles in African rhythm / Gary Stewart.
    p.   cm.
    Discography: p.
    Includes bibliographical references and index.
    Contents: Soukous chic : Kanda Bongo Man — God of the guitar :
Docteur Nico — Toujours O.K. : Franco and l'Orchestre O.K. Jazz —
Ubongo man : Remmy Ongala — The palm wine picker : S.E. Rogie — A
vanishing breed : Big Fayia — Graceland's heartbeat : Francis
Fuster —Dance the highlife : Nana Ampadu — High Times, hard times
: Hedzoleh Soundz — The beat goes on : Olatunji — The dawn of afro-
beat : Orlando Julius Ekemode — Soul brother number one : Joni
Haastrup — An African musican : Fela Anikulapo-Kuti — Politics
and papa's land : Sonny Okosuns.
    ISBN 0-226-77405-8. — ISBN 0-226-77406-6 (pbk.)
    1. Popular music—Africa—History and criticism. 2. Musicians—
Africa—Biography. I. Title.
ML3502.5.S73   1992
781.63'096—dc20   91-30279
                                                              CIP
                                                              MN

⊗ The paper used in this publication meets the
minimum requirements of the American National Standard
for Information Sciences—Permanence of Paper for
Printed Library Materials, ANSI Z39.48-1984.

For Beth Raps

"Success" often brings, in its train, a lot of depressing consequences, because there seems to be something in the process of acquiring a certain degree of success that involves the one crucial compromise that somehow eliminates that elusive quality that attracted you in the first place.

John Peel, BBC disc jockey

Contents

Acknowledgments

It was in Freetown, Sierra Leone, in 1970 that I bought my first African records. My friend Sammy Kamara, then around twelve years old, led me along bustling Goderich Street to Adenuga's record shop, where, at his urging, I purchased two 45s by S. E. Rogie. For the previous two years, African pop music had been insinuating itself into my consciousness as I worked as a Peace Corps volunteer in Sierra Leone's Northern Province, and I wanted to take some of it along as I returned to the United States. My expanding interest in African music, and ultimately this book, stem from Sammy's infectious enthusiasm for the pop music of his home.

Over the years since then, I've had the good fortune to meet and interview many of Africa's finest musicians, most notably those profiled in this book. I am grateful for their friendship and willingness to talk freely about their lives and their music. In addition to those featured here, I would like to thank the late Dessouin Bosuma, Gerry Dialungana, Diblo Dibala, Doctor Dynamite, Sam Mangwana, Dizzy Mandjeku, the late Isaac Musekiwa, Kenneth Okulolo, and Tabu Ley Rochereau for giving of their time and knowledge in response to my questions.

Special thanks go to Ibrahim Kanja Bah of the African Music Gallery in Washington, D.C. Ibrahim arranged for me to meet the late Docteur Nico and Tabu Ley and acted as interpreter during my interviews with these two pioneers of modern Congo music. He is the most knowledgeable person I have ever met on the subject of African music, and lucky for me he loves to talk about it. The contributions of Sasu Adjivon, Joe Boyd, Akie Deen, Chris During, Mickey Hart, Stanley Kabia, Stewart Levine, Nsala Manzenza, Emmanuel Nado, Abu Sillah, Douglas Smith (DMS Communication Design), Elizabeth Sobo, and Sarah Weston (Paul Simon's office) were also immensely helpful to this project.

Beth Raps, linguist extraordinaire, translated two books and several articles from French into English for me during the course of my research and acted as my translator, editor, and proofreader as the manuscript took shape. Erika Steffer interpreted during some of my interviews with members of O.K. Jazz. The producers of Toronto's annual Afro-Fest, Thaddeus Ulzen and Sam Mensah, paved the way for my interviews with Kanda Bongo Man and Sonny Okosuns. Jody Boulting, the world's greatest road manager, made me a member of Kanda's entourage for two exciting days, and Ekua Ulzen acted as translator for my interview with him.

Thanks also to Andrew Seidenfeld of Shanachie Records for helping to arrange my interview with Fela; to Naomi Ware for her hilarious good humor and access to her pristine collection of African records; to Kaye Whiteman and his successors Onyema Ugochukwu and Ad' Obe Obe of *West Africa* magazine for publishing some of these profiles in their first rudimentary form; and to C. C. Smith, editor of *The Beat*, America's leading publication on African music, and editor Richie Unterberger of *Option* magazine for likewise getting the first incarnations of some of these profiles into print.

Finally, thanks and love go to my parents Alan and Harriet Stewart, my brother Alan, and my dear friends Tony Smith, Sam Taylor, and Christine Nelson for their help and encouragement as I stumbled into a writing career; and gratitude to T. David Brent, senior editor at the University of Chicago Press, for shepherding my manuscript through the acquisitions process and seeing it into this final form.

Introduction

The musical monotony of the big five multinational recording companies is slowly beginning to erode. With dogged persistence, third world music keeps nipping at the heels of the stodgy conglomerates. Powerful messages from Bob Marley and Jimmy Cliff propelled reggae into the world's consciousness. Today, the sinewy guitars and polyrhythmic percussion of African music are making similar inroads. We hear soukous and afro-beat on the radio. African bands tour Europe and America. Pop stars like Paul Simon, Peter Gabriel, and Mick Fleetwood perform with African musicians and incorporate African rhythms and arrangements in their music. And perhaps most telling of all, the handful of small independent labels—Original Music, Rounder, Shanachie, and Carthage (now part of Rykodisc)—that helped introduce African music in the United States have lately been joined by some of the ever so timid majors, such as Polygram through its Mango and Island labels and WEA with Virgin and Warner Brothers.

Breakout is pop music jargon for a recording on the road to becoming a hit. To break out is precisely what African musicians are trying to do as they struggle to be heard in the world market. There is much to be learned from their efforts; this book tells some of the story. It explores four major musical styles, soukous, highlife, afro-beat, and palm wine, through the lives of artists from Zaire, Ghana, Nigeria, and Sierra Leone. Theirs are stories not only of music but of politics, economics, and social upheaval as rural economies suddenly became urban and captive nations drove for independence.

By the time the twentieth century arrived, African life had been profoundly distorted by the holocaust that was the slave trade and the continent's continued exploitation under European colonialism. For much of Africa, growth of popular music styles reflects the processes of dislocation and modernization inflicted on its people. Choral hymns of Christian missionaries, brass bands of military garrisons, folk songs of merchant seamen sailing from port to port all contributed to their development. So too did the arrival of foreign instruments, most notably cheap acoustic guitars, and the

1

revolution in technology with its new inventions—radios, gramophones, records, and eventually tape recorders and amplified instruments. These electronic gadgets from the industrialized West
helped spread musical forms around the world.

The growth of Africa's cities was another crucial element in the
development of its popular music. Spurred by improvements in education, political pressure for Africanization of business and government, and worldwide economic expansion following World
War II, Africa's population became increasingly urban. Large numbers of mostly young people left their farms to search for alternative
employment and a "modern" way of life.

Expanding cities became melting pots that fostered the breakdown of traditional ethnic ties. New forms of entertainment
crossed cultural boundaries. Musicians blended elements from the
wide array of musical forms flowing into urban areas. The soukous,
highlife, afro-beat, and, to a lesser extent, palm wine sounds of
West and Central Africa all evolved within this burgeoning urban
milieu.

Not surprisingly, African pop is closely connected to the music
of black and Latin America. "Africans," writes music historian John
Storm Roberts, "far from arriving in the New World without any
cultural baggage, not only brought a great deal with them but
planted it so well that it took root and grew profusely."[1] The music
that evolved under their influence—the blues, jazz, and rock main-
stays of twentieth-century Western culture along with the myriad
of styles from Latin America—managed something that most of its
creators never did; riding on radio and records, it made its way back
to the motherland.

Highlife music of forties and fifties dance bands borrowed heavily from jazz. Listening to old recordings of Ghana's "king of highlife" E. T. Mensah, one can almost picture the group on a nightclub
stage in Harlem or Chicago in the 1930s. When Louis Armstrong
visited the Gold Coast (now Ghana) in 1956, he was greeted by an
all-star band playing a song popularized by Mensah called "All for
You." Correspondent Iain Lang reported that Armstrong "immediately recognized this as the tune of a Creole song he used to hear
in New Orleans half a century ago. Had it been brought to Accra,
perhaps by a coloured seaman off an American freighter? Or had an

old African melody survived in the Gold Coast and on the Gulf Coast?"[2]

In Central Africa, originators of the budding Congo music style (what we now call soukous) incorporated the word *jazz* into the names of their bands. Borrowing again, this time from the Caribbean, Franco's O.K. Jazz and Joseph Kabasele's African Jazz built their music on the beat of the Cuban rumba, a rhythm that had its roots back in Africa.

To a man, the younger artists profiled here acknowledge the influences of African-American music and its white derivatives. James Brown, Chuck Berry, Elvis Presley, Cliff Richard, and the Beatles inspired a generation of African musicians. Joni Haastrup

DMS Communication Design / San Francisco

remembers that during his high school days in Nigeria, "we all started doing this Beatles hair. I mean, this hair [tugs at his own] is so unmanageable, but we really somehow tried to make it cover our face like the Beatles."[3]

Hollywood and its European counterparts were another source of inspiration. Sonny Okosuns recalls that in Nigeria "we watched *Tommy Steele Story*, then Cliff Richard's *Expresso Bongo*. . . . I saw Elvis's *Loving You* and *Love Me Tender*. That's when I decided I would like to be like Elvis. I would like to be a musician."[4] Other films to stir imaginations were *The Young Ones* with Cliff Richard and the Shadows, an Italian movie about the Caribbean called *Calypso*, *Rock around the Clock* featuring Bill Haley and the Comets, and *Twist around the Clock* with Chubby Checker.

Waves of Western music washing over African shores gave rise to the expression *copyright*. Not the legal term, *copyright* instead refers to the propensity of many bands for covering recordings from abroad. In the words of Joni Haastrup, "We just bought music sheets, and just take everything note for note, chord for chord, and play it." Dozens of bands, including Haastrup's Clusters and the Heartbeats of Francis Fuster, built their reputations playing copyright.

If exotic sounds and sights stimulate youthful fantasies, parental disapproval often nips them in the bud. At best, musicians in Africa are regarded as little more than beggars. At worst, they are seen as degenerate purveyors of immorality, especially among parents who sacrifice their own wants to educate their children. As we shall see in the stories to come, those who wish to play music often have to do it in secret or leave home.

Women suffer the dual impediments of parental veto and their secondary status in Africa's largely male-dominated societies. The "woman's place is in the home" syndrome that Western women have fought to remedy still thrives within Africa's well-entrenched patriarchy. An independent woman making it in the music business is a rarity. Those who succeed are usually relegated to roles as backup singers or dancing girls in skimpy costumes adorning a stage dominated by the male star. There are exceptions—Onyeka Onwenu of Nigeria, and Zaireans M'bilia Bel, Tshala Muana, and Abeti come to mind—but popular music in the four countries considered here remains, for the most part, the creation of men.

In the two decades from the midfifties to the midseventies, music in Africa was a thriving cottage industry. All it took to make a record was a little capital and a microphone hooked to a one- or two-track reel tape recorder. Local businessmen set up scores of small, often one-shot, independent record labels. Tapes were sent to London or Paris or Brussels for pressing into 78 RPM records and, later, seven-inch 45s. European record companies like Decca and EMI also recorded African musicians to cater to the new and potentially lucrative markets of educated, employed, urban residents. Record shops sprang up. Inexpensive portable record players were plentiful. Pop bands multiplied.

While the music flourished in Africa, little of it was heard outside the continent. A few groups made forays into Europe and America, where small quantities of records were circulated among immigrant Africans and a cult of non-African enthusiasts. But for the most part, the music remained an African phenomenon.

Beginning in the late seventies, however, the picture started to change. Most African economies began an inexorable slide into depression pushed along by the continuing abandonment of rural areas (which meant decreased farm production and increased food imports), rising petroleum prices (in the case of Nigeria, oil boom followed by oil bust), worldwide recession, chronically depressed raw materials prices, and large-scale corruption within governments. The resulting scarcity of foreign exchange to finance imports began to debilitate the pop music industry, which is dependent on equipment manufactured in the industrialized West. At the same time, an epidemic of music piracy, fueled by the proliferation of cheap cassettes and recording machines, raced across the continent purloining profits and dampening artistic spirits.

Feeling the economic pinch, many musicians began to look more seriously at markets elsewhere. Like their Western counterparts, African musicians want to be seen and heard by the largest possible audience. The lure of modern facilities and big money abroad is powerful. The apparently glamorous and affluent lifestyle of an international pop star is something many aspire to. But how does one break out?

Some, like Fela, Nana Ampadu, and Sonny Okosuns, have chosen to base themselves at home, build a reputation locally, then tour abroad on the strength of their homegrown popularity. Others, like Kanda Bongo Man and S. E. Rogie, have successfully pursued careers abroad despite the built-in disadvantages of working in an alien environment and challenging its established musical mores. Still others, like Hedzoleh Soundz, remain abroad in the face of diminished prospects, driven perhaps by shame and pride, to chase an ever more elusive dream.

Regardless of the obstacles, foreign cities are becoming the capitals of African music. London, Paris, and New York are, if not permanent homes, at least the business addresses of a growing number of African musicians. This movement has spread the music's popularity in Europe and America and transformed Western entertainment centers into hotbeds of musical experimentation.

"It's not that African music will take over and dominate, but it creates an international music," says a hopeful Ibrahim Bah of Washington's African Music Gallery. "There will not be just one mainstream music, but the best of each style will gain recognition for what it is."[5] Producer Stewart Levine echoes the sentiments: "I think world music just generally is going to be all over the place in the nineties. I don't think you're going to have any real movement unless it's got some sort of influence from the third world."[6]

What follows are stories from one corner of the third world. They are stories of Africans, famous and not so famous, and their contributions to the world of music.

Soukous Chic

Kanda Bongo Man

The hype is refreshingly minimal. A low-key announcement, and there before us stands the star almost as if he'd wandered in with the curious crowd. Drumsticks click—one, two, three. A cymbal cracks, a guitar rings out, a bass kicks in. A flashy two-woman, two-man front line swaggers in time before the microphones. The crowd sways involuntarily, suddenly intoxicated by the sensory rush.

Kanda Bongo Man, rakish in loose-fitting designer clothes and trademark round-brimmed, flat-topped hat, shimmies up to the mike as if propelled by the music's energy. The Bongo Man has come. A night of soukous begins to sizzle.

This time it's Toronto, next to the last stop on a thirteen-city North American tour. Before that it was London and Paris and Ouagadougou. Soon it will be Dakar and Banjul. Soukous is hot and so is Kanda Bongo Man.

Zairean-born Kanda is one of a new generation of purveyors of the infectious pop music known to millions of Africans for over a quarter century as "Congo music." While rock and rollers in the West were doing the chicken and the stroll, urban youth in the twin Congos (one of which would later become Zaire) were dancing to rumba-based creations like the boucher, soukous, kiri kiri, and—later, as astronauts landed on the moon—apollo. When Congo music began to penetrate the realm of Western pop in the early eighties, record industry promoters, with their passion for classification and labeling, seized on soukous as an appropriate appellation.

To Kanda Bongo Man's way of thinking, soukous is as good a label as any. It's Friday morning after a Thursday night show, and Kanda is making himself a peanut butter sandwich at the table in

7

his Toronto hotel room. Speaking in French, he excuses himself and says it will be just a few minute before he can answer interview questions. He's dressed casually in dark slacks and a blue sweatshirt littered with slogans, a sharp contrast to his stylish stage attire.

Most of today's soukous stars, and many of their fans, have come to be known as *sapeurs* (society of ambiancers and persons of elegance)—people who consider style and fashion to be nearly as important as the music. Some musicians design their own clothes; others patronize the couturiers of France and Italy and even Japan in an effort to outdo their competitors. While Kanda won't admit to being a sapeur, onstage he and his troupe are splendidly dressed. His is a show of equal parts sight and sound, both of them dazzling.

Kanda was his father's name. Bongo Man, he swears, was his grandfather's. "There are many English influences in our language, for example *man* and *me*," he explains.[1] His grandfather played hand drums, so people called him Bongo Man. "I'm from a family of musicians," he says. So his parents, not a public relations firm, gave him his distinctive handle.

He was born in 1955 in Inongo, Bandundu Province, west central Belgian Congo, during the era of Joseph Kabasele's African Jazz, the band that launched Docteur Nico, Rochereau, and Manu Dibango on the road to stardom. A year later O.K. Jazz, featuring eighteen-year-old Franco, was formed. Kanda grew up with the new urban pop music these pioneers created—a delicious synthesis of traditional melodies, African and Latin rhythms, and a touch of American jazz.

By the time he began to attend boarding school in Kinshasa (known then as Leopoldville), he had already begun to sing in small groups of school friends. Singing was always his first love, and in Kinshasa there were many opportunities. The tiny base of pioneering bands, including African Jazz and O.K. Jazz, that reigned at the time of Kanda's birth had exploded in the next dozen years to number more than thirty.

As Kanda entered his teens, groups like Dynamic Jazz, City Five, Diamant Bleu, and Casanova were challenging their elders. The recording houses—Ngoma, Esengo, Loningisa—that had sprung up in the fifties were working overtime to meet the musical demands of an insatiable audience of young people throughout Africa.

Kanda's favorite band was l' Orchestre Bella Bella, a group that evolved in 1969 from a personnel split within another popular band called Baby National. Fronted by the singing brothers Vangu and Dianzenza Soki, Bella Bella produced a sound Kanda found "inspiring." "Even now when people hear my music, they hear the influences of Bella Bella," he says.

Competition among bands and musicians was fierce, auditions for open positions arduous. "You had to be gifted to make it into a group," Kanda recalls. "It's quite competitive." A little-known group called Tao Tao was the first to make use of teenaged Kanda's sweet, high-pitched voice. As his style and poise developed, he moved on to Bella Mambo and Makoso in the midseventies.

A new generation was taking control of Congo music. Pepe

DMS Communication Design / San Francisco

Kalle and Nyboma were singing with Lipua Lipua. Abeti, one of the few women to make a name, free-lanced with various bands. Josky Kiambukuta joined O.K. Jazz. Vox Africa featured the guitar of Souzy Kasseya. Zaiko Langa Langa formed with Manuaku Waku and Papa Wemba. Kanda moved with his contemporaries, jumping from group to group as better opportunities arose. He even wound up for a time in the late seventies with his inspiration, l' Orchestre Bella Bella.

Apart from the artists' enormous talent, a key ingredient in this flourishing of African pop music was Western technology—cheap radios, record players, electric guitars, and recording equipment. But by the midseventies serious economic decline and the dizzying pace of technological improvements in recording equipment combined to undermine the local recording industry. African record labels were competing directly with imported works of Western artists for consumers' shrinking pay, so more and more investment was required to keep up to date, to sound as polished and professional as the imports. It was impossible. What little foreign exchange the economies generated went for more essential goods or down the rat hole of political corruption. Studio owners could scarcely maintain the equipment they had.

Squeezed by the failing economies, discouraged over deteriorating studios, musicians of Congo and Zaire began moving abroad, especially to Paris. Among them, in 1979, was Kanda Bongo Man. "It's extremely difficult to survive there," Kanda says of his homeland. "The facilities aren't good. And it's very difficult and expensive, for instance, to live in Kinshasa and go to Paris just to do one's recordings." But living in Paris wasn't any easier. The image of Western riches and stardom was shattered by the reality of an immigrant's struggle. Kanda was reduced to working odd jobs and singing in little clubs in order to survive.

After nearly three years of drudgery, he began to benefit from his persistence. A small Paris label, Afro Rythmes, signed him to record his first solo album. *Iyole,* released in 1981, began Kanda's collaboration with Diblo Dibala, one of this era's best soukous lead guitarists. Mislabeling of the songs—they don't appear in the order indicated—didn't detract from the promise of the music. He followed up the next year with *Djessy,* another Afro Rythmes re-

Soukous Chic: Mimi Kazidonna, Remy Salohmon, Pierre Belkos, and Kanda Bongo Man

Kanda Bongo Man

lease featuring Diblo and Shaba Kahamba, longtime bassist for l'Orchestre Bella Bella.

Kanda's music is a lively, marvelous bacchanal that rouses audiences and sends them streaming to the dance floor. The rhythm is built on a sizzling snare drum intertwined with the kick drum's steady "thump, thump." A bass guitar lopes along in the background. "Rumba remains the root of Congolese music, of soukous," Kanda says. "We change a little, we adapt and so on, but that rumba influence is really the root, it's the base."

He adds to that two guitars, a lead—usually Diblo or another gifted player, Dally Kimoko—to carry the melody, and a rhythm. The style is that perfected by the late Docteur Nico and his brother Déchaud in the days of African Jazz and African Fiesta. The guitars play at the same time but skillfully never intrude on each other's territory. The interplay is lean and crisp, a ringing, pulsating sound unlike anything heard in Western musical genres. He often adds a third guitar called the mi-solo, an innovation common to soukous, that gingerly crisscrosses its way through the other two.

Flourishing along the top of it all are the smooth, high-pitched, Lingala and French harmonies of Kanda and two or three backup singers. "My music is about love and everyday life—I have no politics whatsoever," he told writer James Marck, perhaps expressing a disposition formed during his early life under repressive regimes back home.[2]

Iyole and *Djessy* triggered the breakthrough Kanda had been working toward. For one thing, the records sold. Promoters began calling, among them representatives of London's 1983 WOMAD (World of Music, Arts and Dance) festival—a booking that produced widespread critical acclaim for Kanda. England's Globestyle Records started talking about a deal that eventually led to the LP *Non Stop Non Stop*, a compilation of tracks licensed from Afro Rythmes. More important, he began to earn enough money to produce his own albums. "I prefer to be a musician as well as a producer," he says. "I want to be in control of the final product."

The first release on his independent Bongo Man label was the 1984 LP *Amour Fou*. A customarily upbeat collection, the album features Diblo's memorable guitar solos and for the first time introduces a synthesizer into the mix. Kanda pays tribute to his old

Diblo Dibala

groups Bella Mambo and Bella Bella with a nice track called "Bella-Bella Elombe."

His albums come together in a fashion typical of the Paris African music scene. "Right now, all the great francophone African musicians live in Paris," he says. They are a community of free-lancers. When one has a project, he selects those he wants to play with and they go into the studio. The principal artist gets the royalties, the others a onetime payment.

Kanda prepares his compositions—he writes all his own material—then drafts from among Paris-resident virtuosos like Diblo, Kimoko, and fellow guitarists Rigo Star and Lokassa Ya Mbongo, drummers Domingo Salseros and Ty-Jan, bass players Andre "Du Soleil" Kinzonzi and Pablo Lubadika. In turn, he participates in other projects, contributing lead and background vocals on many albums including those by Rigo Star, Pepe Kalle, and Nyboma.

Amour Fou was followed in 1985 by *Malinga,* a work of equal kick and quality. Its most remarkable element is the song "J.T.," an enthralling, energetic groove. Halfway through the guitar solo, Diblo rockets into a tantalizing, repetitious hook that sends shivers climbing up the spine.

Among those impressed was Joe Boyd, owner of England's Hannibal Records and its American counterpart, Carthage, labels that started out reissuing the back catalogs of Richard Thompson and Fairport Convention and branched out from there into whatever areas struck Boyd's fancy. "I saw Kanda about four years ago. . . . in London and was just knocked out," he says.[3] Boyd tracked him down in Paris and arranged to license his music for release in England and the United States. First to be issued was the album *Amour Fou/Crazy Love,* a combination of songs from the original *Amour Fou* and *Malinga.*

A later Hannibal/Carthage release, *Kwassa Kwassa,* combined two of Kanda's other Paris LPs, *Lela Lela* and *Sai. Kwassa Kwassa* celebrates, what else, kwassa kwassa, another dance step in the soukous tradition (*kwassa* is a pun on the French expression "C'est quoi ça?" What's that?). The ten-song album is a fresh, undiluted, high-energy feast performed by the usual stellar cast.

But working abroad has fostered changes, declares Diblo Dibala: "Our music compared to real African music is really changing because of technology."[4] The development of synthesizers, various electronic enhancements, and the digital recording process render works produced in Europe far different from the creations of Kinshasa's outmoded studios. He emphasizes that the African roots are still there, but sometimes it "feels like we have one foot in Africa and one foot in Europe."

For Boyd, Kanda's unswerving fidelity to the basic rumba-based soukous beat is the key to his surging popularity. Contrary to the thinking of many artists and producers, Boyd feels that that constancy is especially important to breaking into Western markets. "I don't think," he says, "that people in America and in Britain and western Europe, they don't go listening to African musicians so that they can hear mid-Atlantic [rock] rhythms."

Kanda isn't above experimenting, however. Witness the incursion of a synthesizer onto some of his tracks. He has also flirted with that palliative of techno-pop enthusiasts, zouk. "It was an adventure," he says of his work with Antillean producer Servais Liso and members of Kassav' on the LP *Zouk Time*. But he emphasizes it was just a onetime thing.

Joe Boyd speaks for many who have experienced the vigor and exuberance of a Kanda Bongo Man show: "I remember being on Kanda's tour and just looking from behind the stage out at the audience, and every single face had an ear-to-ear grin on it. That's what I love about what Kanda does."

Whether that's enough to break African music into mainstream Western pop markets remains to be seen. After all, Boyd points out, most record buyers use music as a sort of soundtrack for their lives. English lyrics about familiar situations will always be more appealing to the majority. "So probably," he says, "the big breakthroughs for African music are going to be when, you know, Tiffany does a soukous record." Perhaps so, but Kanda Bongo Man at least has his foot in the door. He and his contemporaries have taken the torch from the pioneers and brought Congo music to a wider world.

God of the Guitar

Docteur Nico

His parents named him Nicolas Kasanda. A Belgian DJ dubbed him "Docteur." His *nom d'authentique* was Kasanda wa Mikalay. And a generation called him "god of the guitar." Docteur Nico was all of those, but the music he made was simply magic.

Using a spare, one-note picking technique and distinctive tuning scheme, Nico transformed the ordinary guitar into an instrument of enchantment. With crisp, sharp flourishes, bobbing and weaving through his brother Déchaud's steady rhythm guitar accompaniment, he helped to mold and shape the Congo music sound that swept across Africa and burst into Europe in the sixties and seventies.

In early 1985, in the midst of a comeback following several years of relative inactivity, Nico came to Washington, D.C., to negotiate a record deal and obtain treatment for what was termed "a blood disorder." He was a diminutive figure, short and slight of build. Dressed in black nylon parachutist's trousers and a black and white checkered shirt, he perched on the edge of the bed in his hotel suite to answer interview questions while he fooled around with his newest purchase, a guitar shaped like a machine gun. His appearance conjured up images of Ivan O. Martin from *The Harder They Come,* but he was warm and articulate and anxious to talk about his Congo music.

The Congo (now Zaire), a country which would later explode musically and politically, was the Kingdom of the Congo in 1482 when the first Portuguese explorers arrived. A relatively small area around the mouth of the Nzadi (Congo/Zaire) River inhabited by the Bakongo people, its territory would expand enormously with the onslaught of colonialism. By 1908, when it was annexed by Belgium, it encompassed more than two hundred ethnic groups and nine hundred thousand square miles of thick rain forest, broad savanna, and immense mineral wealth—a colony nearly eighty times as large as its metropolis.

It was into this Belgian Congo that Nico was born on July 7, 1939, in a town called Mikalay near Kananga (formerly Luluabourg). Local custom dictated that a child be given the name of an ancestor, so he was called Kasanda after his grandfather with the Christian first name Nicolas. His elder brother, who became known as Déchaud, was called Charles Mwamba after an uncle.

Nico's father played accordion, and his mother was a singer and dancer, so despite parental admonitions to concentrate on school-work, it seemed natural for the two boys to take up music as well. They grew up listening to the pioneers of modern Congo music— Zacharie Elenga, known as Jhimmy, who introduced the Hawaiian guitar style to Congo music, and singer-guitarists Antoine "Wendo" Kolosoi, Henri Bowane, and Léon Bukasa. Nico remembered try-ing to mimic these popular stars with a guitar he had fashioned from a board with nails at each end and a wire strung between.

When traditional life began to disintegrate under the weight of colonialism and the influence of Western missionaries, thousands of Congolese migrated to cities in search of jobs and a "modern" life-style. By the late 1940s urban areas had grown considerably. Nico and Déchaud were among this group of migrants as they moved with their parents to the capital, Leopoldville.

As urban residents found jobs and earned money, consumer goods became affordable; high on the list of desirability were the new technological marvels, radios, gramophones, and records. Within a fairly short span—perhaps a decade or so—the sounds of Europe, America, and, more important for soukous, Latin Amer-ica permeated Congolese cities. African rhythms exported on slave ships suddenly echoed back from 78 RPM record grooves and crackling radio loudspeakers.

The source of Congo music's rhythmic base is a contentious sub-ject among musicians and observers. Did the Congolese borrow from Latin America or are they themselves the creators? On one point there is near unanimity: For Congo music, rumba is the mother rhythm. Where did it come from? Did it develop indepen-dently on both sides of the Atlantic? Fueled perhaps by a certain chauvinism, the debate over these questions is often heated.

Docteur Nico

Docteur Nico himself may have resolved the issue as well as anyone: "Music doesn't have a frontier. . . . There are Cuban songs that resemble African songs. There are African songs that resemble Cuban songs. It is very difficult to make a comparison. There are American songs that resemble African songs. There are African songs that resemble American songs. . . . It is difficult to decide who is copying whom."[1] Along the same lines, music historian John Storm Roberts points out that "in West Africa and the Congo, Cuban music was returning with interest something that had largely come from there anyway, and so there was the most natural of affinities."[2]

Another major development was the opening of the Congo's first recording studio in 1948. Called Ngoma, it was joined in 1950 by two more studios, Opika and Loningisa. These first rudimen-

tary studios, owned by foreign businessmen, were key elements in
the evolution of modern Congo music. Studios could afford to buy
European horns, guitars, and recording machines that were far beyond the financial reach of most Congolese. Musicians hung
around the studios, practicing and recording with the instruments,
exchanging ideas on composition and technique. Their incorpora-
tion of traditional Congolese rhythms and melodies with echoes of
Africa from radio and record created an exciting, modern music
that was joyous and witty and above all highly danceable. The
newly arrived city dwellers embraced it heartily.

It was in this studio atmosphere that Nico got his start. Of
Opika he said, "That's the studio that made me what I am today." It
was just a small one-track affair about as large as a medium-size par-
lor. The musicians would gather around a microphone at one end
of the room, and the owner, a businessman named Gabriel Moussa
Benatar, would operate the recorder at the other end. The tapes
were then sent to London for pressing into 78 RPM records.

Tabu Ley Rochereau, who played with Nico in the sixties, remembers the extraordinary keenness and feeling of those early sessions: "What we'll never be able to recapture is the spontaneity, the
concentration, of the musicians of that era, who made an effort to
know the piece straight through to the end, not to make a mistake.
And out of this sprang stuff, as far as spontaneity goes, that was
unbelievable, which we no longer see."[3]

Oblivious to the financial aspects of the business, the musicians
were thrilled to hear their music on record and were paid little or
nothing for their work. The late saxophonist Isaac Musekiwa, who
played with Nico in the early fifties, remembered that "they were
paying two hundred fifty francs [Belgian francs, approximately five
dollars]. You can be ten [players], you're going to divide that. If
you play alone, it's yours."[4] Royalties were nonexistent. "We didn't
know that," said Musekiwa. "That was after. We didn't know that
when they sell records they've got to earn something. No! Your
name is out. You're known that you are the one who played. You're
happy for that, and that's all."

Whatever money there was to be made came from live performances. Musicians would get together to play for an occasional
party or wedding and, more often, to entertain in bars. Nico re-

membered that in the fifties musicians initially played for a percentage of a bar's drink sales and later began to collect entry fees at the door.

Nico made his first recording at Opika singing with Jhimmy and Paul Mwanga, a popular singer of the time. Benatar took a liking to "little Nico" and bought him a guitar and a bicycle for encouragement. Nico turned to Déchaud, who had become proficient enough to win a spot as Jhimmy's accompanist, for guitar instruction. He practiced constantly to develop his style and technique.

In the early fifties there were no permanent bands in the Belgian Congo. A musician would simply call on his friends to back him when he had a song to record or a wedding to play for—an arrangement similar to that prevailing among today's soukous musicians in Paris. As his guitar skills improved, Nico was often asked to accompany others like Jhimmy, Mwanga, and an up-and-coming singer named Joseph Kabasele. Nico, Déchaud, and Kabasele, along with bass player Albert Toumani and guitarist Tino Baroza, played together so much that they decided in 1953 to become a permanent group. Nico, a short, slightly built teenager at the time, was dubbed "Nico Mobali" (Nico the real man) by his fellow musicians, and Kabasele was known as "Kallé Jeef" and "le Grand Kallé." With a nod to the music of black America, they called their group African Jazz.

Musekiwa, who joined the band in 1954, recalled that Nico was too young to play publicly at first. "Nico was at the school. He was not playing [publicly]. No, he was playing [on] the records, privately. I was a driver and a saxophone player, and when it's time for Nico to come from the school, I would go over there with a car, to hide the car somewhere. When he comes out with friends, then he change [clothes], and I take my car [to] the other side, enter in the car, and we go to the studio. That's how we started with the band, with African Jazz. . . . After that, when he got a certificate from the school, now he started playing publicly."

L' Orchestre African Jazz created excitement in Leopoldville. The group's records sold well, and people flocked to see its live performances. Kallé's sonorous voice and Nico's inspired guitar produced a sound that seemed to capture the essence of the new urban life. Kallé emerged as the group's agent and producer, and Nico handled the musical arrangements. Around 1955 Nico and

Déchaud dropped their acoustic guitars in favor of electric models. Conga player Antoine "Depuissant" Kaya and trumpeter Willy Kuntima joined the band, and it began recording at the new Esengo studio, a move that led to a brief but creative collaboration in 1958 with a group called Rock-A-Mambo led by Lando Rossignol and Nino Malapet.

While African Jazz was blossoming in the Belgian Congo, the clamor for independence sweeping across Africa bore fruit in the Gold Coast. There, in 1957, the independent nation of Ghana was born. Ghana was followed by Guinea in 1958, and the independence movement gained momentum. The Congolese, frustrated by racism, lack of educational opportunity, and the absence of political and economic freedom, pressured Belgium for independence through clandestine nationalist organizations. As the unity of the colonial establishment unraveled, Belgium relented and agreed to negotiate a timetable for granting independence.

A round-table conference between Belgian and Congolese leaders began in Brussels in January of 1960, and an all-star band was put together to provide entertainment. Nico, Kallé, Déchaud, and maracas player Roger Izeidi were chosen from African Jazz; singer Victor "Vicky" Longomba and bassist Antoine "Brazzos" Armando came from the rival band O.K. Jazz; and a conga player known as Petit Pierre rounded out the group. They entertained the conferees and played public concerts in Brussels and Paris. Nico was particularly impressive. Europeans were amazed to see an African play the guitar with such style and command. Nico remembered that a Belgian radio announcer named Mimi was so taken by his performance she called him "Docteur." A title to match the distinction of the artist was conferred.

With its business complete, the conference adjourned at the end of February, and the delegates headed home to jockey for power. Back in Leopoldville Docteur Nico and the other members of African Jazz basked in the afterglow of their own European triumph. To celebrate their country's approaching independence they released two new records, "Independence Cha Cha" and "Table Ronde," which were instant hits in the last days of the Belgian Congo.

Independence day, June 30, 1960, was a day of celebration throughout the country. Joseph Kasavubu was sworn in as president, and Patrice Lumumba took the oath as prime minister. "*Nous ne sommes plus vos macaques!* (We are no longer your monkeys)," declared Lumumba, pointedly addressing Belgium's King Baudoin in his speech to the gathering.[5]

From that high point the country rapidly disintegrated into near anarchy and civil war. Congolese soldiers rebelled against their white officers, who had fully intended to remain in charge. Belgium responded by sending in troops in a brutal operation, as Europeans fled the country in droves. The mineral-rich province of Katanga seceded in collusion with Belgium, which sought to protect its mining interests. Peacekeeping forces of the United Nations were dispatched to try to maintain order, while rival Congolese factions set up governments in their respective strongholds. In January of 1961 Patrice Lumumba was assassinated—the result of a plot inspired in part by the CIA—and the crisis deepened.[6]

During this period Docteur Nico, who had earned his secondary school certificate in mechanics, was pressed into service as a technical college teacher to replace a European instructor who had fled the country. But in spite of the turmoil, music continued to flourish in the capital, and Nico maintained his career with African Jazz.

Three new additions bolstered the band in 1961: Cameroonian saxophonist Manu Dibango, whom the group had met in Brussels; a new singer, Pascal Tabu, who would become known as Tabu Ley Rochereau; and the itinerant singer-composer Joseph "Mujos" Mulamba. Fonior, a Belgian company that owned the African record label, negotiated a deal with Kallé to record the band and release its records internationally.

In early 1963, however, as the Katanga secession was coming to an end, a secession was brewing within the ranks of African Jazz. Nico and others had become disenchanted with Kallé's handling of the group's affairs. The recording contract with Fonior was an especially contentious issue. Nico remembered that it called for the musicians to fly to Brussels periodically, where they would record up to a hundred songs—the equivalent of fifty 78 or 45 RPM records—in two weeks' time. They were paid only ten thousand francs total (about two hundred dollars) plus transportation and lodging for their work. "They wanted a lot of merchandise," Nico said with great understatement.

Rochereau remembers that most of the songs for such sessions were done on the fly. "The plan was for us to go record in Europe on a somewhat more sophisticated sound board. And he [the company representative] tells you, 'You're here for a week; you will make fifty songs, please. You don't make fifty songs, we won't pay you at all.' On coming out of Zaire we have sometimes five or six songs already prepared, or ten songs. But the [remaining] forty are made on site in the studio. . . . Every single one done in the middle of recording just like that. We're done, okay, okay, okay, let's start composing. And then the technician takes a reel [of tape]. He puts it on the machine, the white technician. It turns, he sleeps. You stop, it turns. You start up, it turns. The finished tape, even if we have nothing on it, he sets it aside. That one's done. He takes another reel. He puts it on. It turns."

The dispute over recording money came to a head in midyear, and the group expelled Kallé. After a brief existence as African Jazz Nico, the band disintegrated when Nico and most of the others, including Déchaud, Rochereau, Izeidi, Mujos, and Depuissant, abandoned African Jazz to form l'Orchestre African Fiesta. The new band was an immediate success with hits like "Fiesta Kombo ya Sika" and "Mama Ege"; unfortunately they did not fare any better when it came to negotiating a recording contract. All the bands of the day were forced into a take-it-or-leave-it decision. If they didn't like one record company's offer, there were no better terms elsewhere. So after a brief, two-year existence African Fiesta split up, with money once again playing a major role. Disagreement between Nico and Izeidi, who acted as the group's agent, was particularly heated. Nico's faction, which included Déchaud, formed a new group called Docteur Nico and Orchestre African Fiesta, while Rochereau and Izeidi formed African Fiesta National. Some, like Mujos and Depuissant, left to join other bands.

African Fiesta was splitting up, but the country itself was slowly coming together. Consolidation in the political arena had been an arduous and painful five-year process, the culmination of which was the seizure of power in a military coup d'etat by General Joseph Mobutu (now President Mobutu Sese Seko) on November 24, 1965. Mobutu began removing reminders of the unhappy past when, in 1966, he changed the name of several major cities including Leopoldville, which became Kinshasa.

Kinshasa's musical community continued to expand, and more

and more groups formed. Musicians and their fans fell, for the most part, into two distinct schools, those who preferred Docteur Nico's progressive sound and others who favored the more traditional style of Franco. François Luambo, known as Franco, had helped to form O.K. Jazz in 1956, and he and Nico were intense competitors. Even in 1985 Nico bristled when asked a question about his rival. The two had occasionally taunted each other in their songs, although in later years the rhetoric cooled. Nico added the word *sukisa,* which is essentially the imperative *stop,* to the name of his band, implying that the other bands should stop bragging because "African Fiesta is the best!"

Docteur Nico and his Orchestre African Fiesta enjoyed an incredible ten-year reign as one of Africa's most popular bands. They recorded hundreds of songs and entertained thousands at live performances across Africa and Europe. Nico introduced the Hawaiian steel guitar into the music and popularized a new dance step called the kiri kiri, which supplanted the soukous. Despite the appearance of success, however, he apparently earned very little money for his work. Record royalties, he claimed, were almost nonexistent, and live performances did little more than keep food on the table.

In 1971 President Mobutu declared that the Democratic Republic of the Congo would henceforth be known as the Republic of Zaire. Early the next year even more far-reaching changes were announced. All citizens with foreign-sounding names were ordered by law to change them to Zairean ones.[7] Most people responded enthusiastically to the *recours á l'authenticité,* and Nicolas Kasanda, remembering his birthplace, became Kasanda wa Mikalay. After a brief period of confusion, musicians were allowed to keep their stage names. "Docteur Nico" continued to reign.

But by the midseventies, fortune took a turn for the worse. Fonior ran into tax problems in Belgium that forced the company to close down when its assets were sold to settle the debt. Docteur Nico was left without a record company. Since he had never been happy with his recording contracts, he said he just decided to "sit back" for a while until the right deal came along. Rumors about drinking and marital problems began to circulate, and there was talk of his declining health, but Nico, who was very guarded about his personal life, insisted he was only waiting for the right opportunity. In view of later events, however, it seems likely the rumors had at least a grain of truth to them.

Nico began to stage a vigorous comeback in 1983 with the assistance of B. G. Akueson, who was then artistic director of the Office Togolais du Disque in Lomé, Togo. At Akueson's behest Nico, Déchaud, and some of their past collaborators traveled to Togo and began recording with Abeti's band, les Redoutables, at the Africa New Sound studio. During the next eighteen months, Nico said, they recorded enough material for ten albums, and tracks were laid in Paris for an additional two. *Dieu de la Guitare (No. 1)* and *Aux USA* were both results of those sessions.

Whether this final flurry of activity was spurred by a premonition or even direct knowledge of his impending fate we will never know. When he came to Washington Nico appeared healthy, and the doctors treating his blood disorder did not feel the condition warranted his hospitalization. He did interviews for Voice of America and concluded a record deal with the African Music Gallery, which eventually released an LP under the title *Adieu*. When he returned to Kinshasa, however, his health began to deteriorate. As the months passed it was decided—it is said by President Mobutu himself—to send him to Belgium for treatment, but by then it was too late. Docteur Nico died in a Brussels hospital on September 22, 1985, at the age of forty-six.

Toujours O.K.

Franco and l'Orchestre O.K. Jazz

3

"Il est mort," say French speakers when a man dies. In the fall of 1989 they said it about another great figure in Zairean music, the leader of O.K. Jazz, Luambo Makiadi, "Franco." He of rounded frame and booming voice, of flashing fingers against strings of steel, vigorous, robust, the picture of life, died in Brussels at the age of fifty-one.

He was called "the grand master," and it was true. One of the pioneers of modern Congo music, he recorded more than one hundred albums and an uncountable number of singles. His ability to capture listeners—with words for those who understood Lingala or French and with an uncanny musical sensibility for those who didn't—coupled with a healthy dose of business acumen fashioned and sustained the seemingly perpetual music machine that was O.K. Jazz.

But Franco's three decades atop the world of African music came to a sad and stunning halt. The good life that fueled his rapidly expanding girth took its toll. In the last year of his life his weight plummeted. He failed to show up in March 1989 for a much-heralded reunion with his former singer Sam Mangwana at London's Hammersmith Palais,[1] and he missed the band's American tour that summer.

The truth of his illness is hard to come by. Close associates, band manager Nsala Manzenza and artistic director Dizzy Mandjeku, claimed he suffered from kidney and stomach ailments.[2] Rumors said he had AIDS. In an interview for *Africa International* quoted in the Paris newspaper *Libération,* Franco denied them: "You know in Zaire, as soon as you're sick everyone yells AIDS. Whether it is cancer, malaria or dysentery, the rumors fly. 'Hey, did you see so-and-so, did you see how skinny he's gotten? Oh, it's AIDS.'

Whereas you could have another disease that's just as dangerous. As for me, I don't have AIDS. It's true that I've gotten a lot thinner and that I now weigh less than 100 kilos [about 220 pounds] whereas I have weighed up to 130 kilos [290 pounds], but the doctors have told me I have a kidney disease. I'm taking care of myself accordingly, and things are going well."[3]

Life's precariousness was hardly a matter for concern back in 1956 when Franco was something of a prodigy at the Leopoldville recording house of Loningisa. He was eighteen years old and part of a large stable of musicians that included some of the pioneers of modern Congolese music—Henri Bowane, Paul "Dewayon" Ebengo, Dessouin Bosuma, Vicky Longomba, and Lando Rossignol, all from the Belgian Congo, and Daniel "De La Lune" Lubelo and Jean Serge Essous from across the river in Congo Brazzaville.

For several years, since around 1953, the Loningisa ensemble had been cranking out records and a tidy profit for the studio's owner, a foreign businessman named Papadimitriou. But in 1956 six of the studio's musicians were hired to play at the O.K. Bar in Leopoldville, and O.K. Jazz was born. On one of their first records, "On Entre O.K. On Sort K.O." (one enters OK, one leaves KO'd), made in late 1956, the band introduces itself. There is Franco on guitar and vocals, Dessouin playing hand drums, De La Lune on bass, clarinetist Essous, and singers Vicky and Rossignol. Dessouin, who died a few months after Franco, recalled that two other Brazzavilleans, Célestin Kouka, who sang and played maracas, and signer Edo Nganga, were original members instead of Essous and Rossignol.[4] Franco's own literature expands the list of names even further.[5] Whatever the case, the six that Dessouin remembered soon became the heart of the band. On the strength of his musicianship and personality Franco emerged as the star.

"Not a pretty boy," wrote journalist Jean-Jacques Kande in 1957, describing the Congo's newest heartthrob. "Slightly taller than the average. Eyes the color of fire, sometimes laughing, sometimes dreaming. Hair cut any which way giving his appearance a very combative air. Very dark black skin. Thus appears the current number one guitarist of the town of Leopoldville, the electric guitarists who makes the hearts of women spin. For them, his name is Franco, from his real name François Luambo. He wears plaid shirts and narrow pants cut cowboy style."[6]

Luambo Makiadi "Franco." Photo courtesy of Ibrahim Bah

Relying heavily on traditional folk elements for inspiration, the members of O.K. Jazz refined and adapted them to fit the capabilities of Western instruments and recording technology. Building on African rhythms and those like the rumba repatriated from Latin America, they translated into song the cares and concerns of the young, rapidly rising Congolese urban class. As Kande, echoing the thoughts of many of his readers, put it, passionate love songs like "Elo Mama" and "Naboyi yo Te" "take you by the throat, twist your heart, electrify you."[7]

Where Joseph Kabasele's African Jazz was developing the mulifarious guitar sound of Nico, Déchaud, and Tino Baroza, O.K. Jazz blended a single guitar with a saxophone. Isaac Musekiwa, a saxophonist from Southern Rhodesia (now Zimbabwe), joined the band in 1957 following a stint with Kabasele's African Jazz. "I was playing the first part," he recalled a few months before his death in early 1990, "and Franco was playing the second part on guitar. Guitar and sax."[8] Sometime in 1958, Angolan guitarist Antoine "Brazzos" Armando was added, and O.K. Jazz began to refine its own strain of guitar interplay.

Politics—independence and the Congolese civil war—heavily influenced the band's evolution by forcing personnel changes and providing rich material for new songs. "Lumumba Héros National" praised the country's new prime minister in 1960, and "Liwa ya Lumumba" mourned his assassination a year later. Diplomatic flare-ups periodically drove the Brazzaville musicians back across the river and opened spots for new talent. O.K. Jazz became a virtual music school, accepting, training, or introducing dozens of artists over the years. Sam Mangwana, Wuta Mayi, Antoine "Papa Noël" Nedule, Michel Boybanda, Jean "Kwamy" Mossi, Mateta "Verckys" Kiamuangana, Joseph "Mujos" Mulamba, and Ntesa "Dalienst" Zitani are only a few of the stars who have played with Franco.

Playing with O.K. Jazz was akin to earning a degree. "It's something to be very proud of, because it has such a history," said Mandjeku shortly before Franco's death. To join the band was "not difficult," he explained. "First of all you must know the work, and second there must be a place open." Most aspirants had to undergo an audition. Either they were asked to perform their own compositions or they played O.K. Jazz standards with members of the band.

Established musicians simply made it known that they wanted to join and were picked up when a slot became available.

Gerry Dialungana's entrance into O.K. Jazz was fairly typical. Born only five years before the band was formed, he grew up admiring the singing voice of Rochereau and teaching himself guitar by mimicking Docteur Nico. "I didn't choose to be a musician," he says, "it just happened."[9] He began playing with neighborhood groups and in 1970 made his professional debut with les Malous. In 1973 he joined Dalienst in les Grand Maquisards; three years later he graduated to O.K. Jazz, where he became a leader in the band's directional committee.

O.K. Jazz was formally organized with Franco as president and a directional committee composed of band members who took responsibility for discipline, rehearsal schedules, equipment, social functions, and general operations. If O.K. Jazz is to continue in existence, it will probably be under the leadership of Franco's vice-president, guitarist Simaro Lutumba.

With such an array of talent, there was never a shortage of material to record. Franco himself was a prolific composer who, according to Mandjeku, liked to get together with a singer to work out a song idea. He would then call in a bass player or another instrumentalist to help complete the composition. If another musician had a song, it would be put on a schedule, and he would audition it for the group. Many songs started as mere skeletons and were developed as collaborative efforts in rehearsal.

"Tradition is a great influence in my music," Franco told Jon Pareles of the *New York Times* in 1983. "In my music I put all my soul, all my spirit, and my soul is a traditional one, because I was born in a family that respected tradition. My mother was always singing traditional songs. The traditional music lacks some sounds, while the modern music has the guitars and the saxophones and many other things. But the spirit of the music is the same."[10]

Despite his close connections to the government of Zaire's President Mobutu—he recorded several songs in support of Mobutu's policies, including "Candidat na Biso Mobutu" (Mobutu is our candidate)—Franco developed a reputation as a spokesman for the people. "Lopango ya Bana na Ngai" (the land of my children) spoke against government land expropriations; "Ngai Marie n'Zoto Ebeba" sings in support of Marie, a Kinshasa prostitute

Founding member of O.K. Jazz Dessouin Bosuma (*left*) and Isaac Musekiwa, who joined the band in 1957

faced with the anger of her clients' wives; "Tailleur" was widely interpreted as a satire on a Zairean prime minister; "Attention na SIDA" warned against the scourge of AIDS. In 1979 Franco and his entire band spent two months in jail for what was ostensibly the offense of performing songs that were deemed by the authorities to be obscene, but at least some observers believed it to be punishment for stretching the boundaries of public criticism of Zaire's ruling class.

Unlike most of his contemporaries, who concentrated mainly on their art, Franco set out to ensure that he and his troops would benefit monetarily from their creations. In the early sixties he established his own publishing house called Epanza Makita to issue records and try to collect royalties. Starting in 1961, he often recorded in Europe for Pathé Marconi and Fonior, and when Fonior folded he established his own labels, Edipop, Visa 1980, and Choc Choc Choc (literally "shock shock shock" in French). He owned Mazadis, a small two-track recording studio in Kinshasa, for many years and was a partner in Zaire's only record pressing plant (both the result of the government's nationalization of foreign-owned businesses in 1974). He even had his own nightclub, the 1-2-3 Club, where the band would play whenever it came to Kinshasa.

Bravado born of success prompted addition of the initials *T.P.*— for *tout puissant,* all-powerful—to the familiar *O.K.* in the early seventies. A decade later the band had grown to become a massive entourage of more than forty people. They were often in such demand that they split into two units to satisfy their commitments.

Music promoter Ibrahim Bah of the African Music Gallery in Washington, D.C., recalls his 1983 experience of bringing the band to the United States for the first time: "I spoke with Franco several times, and we had agreed we were going to have twenty-five people in the group . . . and I applied for the visas and got the visas. A week or so later he got pressure from his quarters that some people must be in the band, and he called me and said, 'Look Ibrahim, I cannot come with just twenty-five, I've got to come with forty-five people.' I said, 'You mean forty-five—four, five?' He said, 'Yes, forty-five.' . . . He gave me the additional names, and I applied [for visas] for the rest of their names. And immigration said, 'Hey, one moment this group is twenty-five, the next minute they're forty-five; what kind of group is this?'"[11] Eventually additional visas were issued, and the tour went ahead despite increased problems of logistics.

The band's songs seemed to lengthen in proportion to its size, although longer songs were actually a result of improved recording technology, changing formats, and the general trend in pop music around the world. The taut two- or three-minute gambols of the early days (dictated by the limits of technology) gave way to extended, laid-back ramblings like "Très Impoli" and "Mario." In live performance the band supercharged its hits into torrid, up-tempo dance-floor grooves worthy of anything produced by the Paris soukous session bands. Fronted by Franco and singers Madilu System and Josky Kiambukuta with support from the sparkling guitars of Simaro Lutumba, Dizzy Mandjeku, Gerry Dialungana, and Thierry Mantuika, T.P.O.K. Jazz was a powerful outfit until Franco's death.

Despite his illness Franco recorded two albums with Sam Mangwana in early 1989, *Franco Joue avec Sam Mangwana* and the wishful, ironic *For Ever,* featuring the track "Toujours O.K." But as his stamina slipped away, work became nearly impossible. There are unconfirmed reports that he managed to play a final date with the band in Brussels only a month before his death. A British music publication described his visit to London three weeks before the end: "The once robust musician had lost a massive amount of weight and conducted interviews lying on his hotel bed. His comments were brief and often bitter, particularly over what he saw as a lack of European interest in African music. Franco seemed upset that no Western artists had seemed interested in working with him."[12]

When death came October 12, President Mobutu declared a period of national mourning in Zaire, and Franco's body was flown home for burial. For the remaining members of T.P.O.K. Jazz, it was a time of sorrow and uncertainty. "From '78 Franco has prepared his band to play without him," Manzenza said in August of 1989, trying to be reassuring about the group's future. "It is an institution," said Mandjeku, pointing to the band's success and longevity. But until that point T.P.O.K. Jazz had never been without Franco.

Ubongo Man

4

Remmy Ongala

At times Remmy Ongala looks like a wild man, his bare chest draped with strings of cowries and assorted amulets, his lower body swathed in brightly colored cloth. A wig of teased grass crowns the carefully braided locks that fall haphazardly about his head. On other occasions he's a Tonton Macoute, sinister, menacing, dread-locks hidden under a wide-brim, flat-top hat, his eyes staking out the crowd from the cover of dark glasses. A T-shirt and khaki trou-sers mold themselves to his well-rounded frame; a guitar rides his protruding belly like a high strung AK-47.

Ongala's looks are striking, but it is his music that commands serious attention. He sometimes strolls onstage alone at the begin-ning of a show, plucking his guitar while introducing the members of his Orchestre Super Matimila as one by one they take the stage to pick up the beat. When the band hits full stride, Ongala begins to sing with a surprising sweetness and clarity. His words, usually in Swahili, ride the repeating guitar riffs, melodious and intense. In a voice that sounds strikingly like Madilu System of T.P.O.K. Jazz, Ongala delivers a lyric as if he owns the words. Whether or not you understand his message, this is clearly a man of passion.

His music is a throwback to the late sixties and early seventies, a rootsy blend of Congo music and the rhythms of East Africa. Lis-ten to Original Music's wonderful oldies collection *The Tanzania Sound*—especially Salim Abdullah with the Cuban Marimba Band, Hodi Boys, National Jazz Band—and some early Franco—perhaps *l'Afrique Danse No. 6* from Sono Disc, which still occasionally pops up in African record bins—and you'll hear where Remmy Ongala and Orchestre Super Matimila are coming from. It's a stripped-down sound, lean and agile, no drum machines or synthesizers or redundant players clogging and suffocating the music, a space for everyone and everyone in his space.

Sounding hauntingly like Franco, Ongala plucks his guitar in a seamless blend with a second lead and accompanying rhythm guitar. Kick drum and congas carry on for a generally absent bass while driving the music in a kind of slowed-down Kenyan-style benga beat.[1] A muted cymbal hisses in double time much as the maracas did two or three decades ago. And a saxophone, the Congolese guitar's most complementary consort, backs and fills and solos.

Ongala calls his music *ubongo,* the Swahili word for brain, because it is "music of the brain; it's heavy thinking music."[2] Since he swings in Swahili, most Westerners must content themselves with the lilting musical quality of his voice. But it helps to know that the words nipping sweetly at our ears have a keen and powerful bite when their meaning is understood. "I sing about things everyone should have in life that will give us all a certain equality," he says. "As for me and my songs, I always go to the world. The world is a prison, because there are . . . people who are proud of their lives and others who are always suffering. . . . I've seen people who had a lot of money and they're all dead. They leave everything here on the earth. Many musicians sing about love, about life. It's always like that. And they don't sing about something that's going to make people [better], [about] what needs to be done to this world. So I try not to sing very much of love, [but] to try to illuminate the situation of the world."

At the time of his birth in 1947, poverty and inequality were wanton in the old Belgian Congo, one of the most severe and exploitative of Europe's African colonies. Ongala's family lived in the eastern part of the country at Kindu, two hundred miles or so west of Lake Tanganyika and the borders of Burundi and Tanzania (although he has also claimed Kisangani some two hundred fifty miles to the north). His beginnings, as he tells it, were extraordinary, a marathon of sorts, both distressing and magical.

Like thousands of other African men who fought for their colonial occupiers during World War II, Ongala's father returned home at war's end, married, and settled back into the life of his country. His wife became pregnant, but the child died. A second pregnancy again ended tragically. In despair his mother went one day to see a local traditional doctor. "So the doctor said it was the same child who arrives each time," Ongala relates. "He said to my mother, 'The next time you are pregnant you mustn't go to a hospital. Come to talk to me, and I'll explain how to have the child.'"

When the time came for her to give birth, she followed the traditional doctor's instructions and delivered the baby, who turned out to be Ongala, in the forest with the doctor in attendance. "I was born feet first with two front teeth. To us, there is a special significance when you are born with two teeth." It is, he explains, almost like an inheritance; one born in such circumstances can become a traditional doctor if he chooses. He was named Ramadhani Ongala Mtoro, and when he decided to become a musician he adopted the title "doctor" in remembrance of his auspicious birth.

The doctor warned Ongala's mother never to cut his hair, an admonition she rigidly followed for fear of losing her thrice-born child. His shaggy locks were a source of shame and ridicule, but his mother remained steadfast. Only once, on her death, did Ongala take a razor to his head. Later, he says with a laugh, "when records by Bob Marley came out, I saw that he had hair like mine. So after that I felt all right. I became proud of my looks."

Music is an integral part of life in Africa; it accompanies the routine as well as the ritual. From the moment of birth Ongala was immersed in it. As a young boy, he quickly learned to play hand drums from his father, who was a traditional singer and drummer. As a teenager in the early sixties, he taught himself to play guitar. The new urban Congo music style was flourishing during his youth. Radio and records brought the sounds of Kinshasa and the rest of the world to even the most remote villages. Ongala loved listening to Cuban records—strange yet familiar African rhythms returning home from across the Atlantic. From Kinshasa rang the golden voice of Joseph Kabasele and the mellow rumba guitar of Franco. These, Ongala fondly recalls, were his primary musical influences.

As his Franco-like guitar picking improved, he began to play professionally, getting gigs with assorted groups at hotels in eastern Zaire and neighboring Uganda. His big break came in 1978 when an uncle living in the Tanzanian capital of Dar-es-Salaam sent for him to come join an ascendant band led by another Zairean,

Mzee Makassy. After nearly three years, he left Makassy to join Orchestre Matimila, a new band he soon made his own.

In the sixties and early seventies Tanzania, like most of the rest of Africa, succumbed to the powerful influence of Congo music. But in the middle to late seventies, while the once prosperous East African Community disintegrated and Tanzania chose to follow the development prescriptions of its charismatic president, Julius Nyerere, in increasing isolation, the music scene in Dar-es-Salaam was transformed.

As the country began to look inward, President Nyerere set up a Ministry of National Youth and Culture to foster local styles of music and dance. But failed development experiments, the shock of rising world oil prices, declining prices for Tanzanian exports, and war with neighboring Uganda, which led to the ouster of the notorious Idi Amin, plunged the Tanzanian economy into decline. Pre-

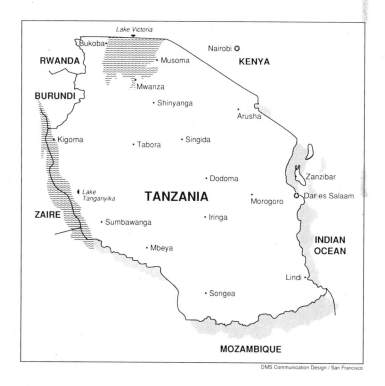

DMS Communication Design / San Francisco

Remmy Ongala

cious foreign currency necessary to finance imports, including musical instruments and recording equipment, began to dry up. A record pressing plant planned in the sixties has yet to be set up although much of its equipment was purchased in the seventies. The Tanzanian Film Company, which is responsible for the country's recording industry, could barely maintain a rudimentary two-track recording studio.[3]

The result has been a largely isolated, but self-contained and even flourishing, local music industry. Radio Tanzania, unable to acquire foreign exchange to purchase imported records, began to stock a tape library of music it recorded with local bands.[4] Live music replaced disco in many urban clubs. Currently in Dar-es-Salaam, Ongala estimates, there are at least twenty bands playing every night. It is within this atmosphere that Orchestre Super Matimila developed.

The band got its name from a small village of a friend of Ongala's and its equipment from a local businessman with enough connections to navigate the country's import laws. They played live shows, as many as five a week, and began to record some of their best songs for Radio Tanzania. In addition to gaining valuable radio air play, the tapes were often sent to neighboring Kenya for pressing into records that in turn spread the band's reputation beyond Tanzania's borders.

But increasing fame failed to yield increasing fortune. "There is no copyright. There are no unions. I'm just beginning to sort that out," Ongala complains. "You send your tape to Kenya to make records, two thousand records. He says to you, 'I'll put a thousand out,' when in fact he's put two thousand out. What can you do?"

What Ongala did was to give one of his tapes to an English friend who was returning to London after visiting Dar-es-Salaam. The friend passed the tape on, and it found its way to WOMAD (World of Music, Arts and Dance). From that chance introduction, Ongala and his band were invited to join the 1988 WOMAD tour; audiences received them with great enthusiasm. At the same time, the WOMAD record label issued an album of some of the group's best radio tapes from the early eighties.

The LP, called *Nalilia Mwana,* is probably Ongala's finest work (liner notes refer to "inferior" sound quality, but that is an unfortunate exaggeration). It includes "Sika ya Kufa," about the death of a fellow musician, "Ndumila Kuwili" (don't speak with two mouths), and "Mnyonge Hana Haki" (the poor have no rights). "I think all time for the poor, like 'Sauti ya Mnyonge'," he says, citing a song that translates as the "voice of the poor" or "underdog" from another LP, *On Stage with Remmy Ongala.*

On record he uses more vocal harmony than in live performance. A second lead and backing vocals appear on several songs. Harmonizing saxophones and even trumpets show up on others. But the sound of Ongala insistently spitting out his message over rolling, repeating, equally insistent guitars dominates the music.

Rave notices for his 1988 work with WOMAD led to the group's inclusion in the 1989 WOMAD tour and a brand-new album, *Songs for the Poor Man,* on WOMAD-affiliated Real World Records. Recorded in England at Peter Gabriel's Real World Studios, *Songs for the Poor Man* is Super Matimila's first work in a modern studio. As always the messages are strong and passionate, as in a remake of "Sauti ya Mnyonge," "Karola," which says "be careful in a world where you believe there is goodness," and the antiracist "Kipenda Roho."

Next to the anguish of poverty, the evil of racism is closest to Ongala's heart. He is married to a white Englishwoman with whom he has three children. "In the world now, it's a new world," he reasons. "We don't have the old world that we had. . . . My children, they're not white and they're not black, they're children. We come from the same father. We're different, but we come from the same place. . . . My children are the children of the whole world. My children are everyone's children. They're not white; they're not black. I can't work with that [racist] system." He sings about it in "Kipenda Roho":

> What the heart loves
> The body follows
> Love has no color
> Love has no race.

And how is his message being accepted in the West? "Why shouldn't it be accepted?" he retorts. Why not indeed. After all, it *is* music for the brain and for the feet and hips as well. If acceptance is not yet total, at least this dreadlocked, consciousness-raising African is beginning to get a hearing.

The Palm Wine Picker

S. E. Rogie

America's formula-driven music industry has been unkind to most African musicians. It beckons with the promise of enormous riches, then rebuffs with a calculated closed-mindedness. S. E. Rogie can attest to that. A major star in West Africa, he left his fame on the shores of the Atlantic to pursue the American dream. But fortune decreed a decade of disappointment before resuscitating the singer in England.

Rogie is Sooliman Ernest Rogers from Fornikoh near Pujehun in southern Sierra Leone. Playing in the folksy palm wine guitar tradition and singing with a smooth baritone, he issues musical warnings, bemoans broken romances, and generally offers advice with songs like "Baby Lef Marah," "Toomus Meremereh nor Good," and "My Lovely Elizabeth." From the midfifties until the early seventies, Rogie was a dominant figure on the music scene in Sierra Leone and beyond.

"Palm wine guitar music is like folk music or blues," he says. "People sing heart-to-heart songs, what they feel. They drink a little to feel happy, and what they drink is palm wine."[1] The wine is sweet milky sap from a variety of palm tree plentiful in West Africa. The music is a blend of rural tradition and urban acculturation. Fortified by the arrival of cheap acoustic guitars, and the musical exchange fostered by sailors plying the waters along the Gulf of Guinea and Sierra Leonean *Krios* (Creoles) who staffed the apparatus of colonialism up and down the coast, it took root in the twenties and thirties. The sailors, many of whom were from the Kru people of Sierra Leone and Liberia, brought sea shanties and records from other lands. Krios, the comparatively well-educated descendants of an amalgam of Africans of varying ethnicity, freed from slavery and repatriated to the colony of Freetown (now Sierra

41

Leone's capital), carried music from post to post throughout British West Africa.

The 1940s found Rogie in the thick of this evolving musical mix. Lacking the funds to attend school, the teenaged Rogie moved to Freetown to learn a trade. He settled in with an elder brother and began work as an apprentice tailor. During the long days of cutting and sewing, he began to meet some musicians who frequented the tailor shop. "One day," he recalls, "I asked one of the guitarists to teach me to play the guitar. So he put my fingers on the guitar and showed me that was [the chord] C, and the whole process lasted about fifteen minutes. . . . That was all the instruction that I had, and I picked it up from there."

As he became proficient at both professions, Rogie was struck with a novel idea; he would combine the two. "Before long I started traveling from place to place playing my guitar," he says. "I would go to a town and open up my tailor shop, you know. I sew all day and the evening I pick up my guitar, entertain people." But whatever money there was to be made came strictly from the tailoring business. "I wasn't making money in the night," he explains, "I was doing it for fun. I was just doing it for enjoyment, get [a] drink and get high, that's all. I wasn't paid for that. I wasn't paid. In those days nobody wants to pay. People just sit around and listen to you sing, buy a little drink for you."

Other more established guitarists influenced Rogie's musical development. He remembers players with names like Joe Boy Nor, Ekundaio, Freddie the Great, Tall Boy, and Slim who usually sang and played guitar accompanied by triangle and maracas. "Those are the exponents of palm wine music in Sierra Leone," Rogie declares. "They actually held the [music's] lifeblood because they played for weddings, they played concerts, they played all kinds of occasions."

Sounds from abroad also provided inspiration. Rogie spent hours with his brother's gramophone and ample record collection, listening, absorbing, the music firing his imagination. He was most taken with the songs and delivery of American country-western singer Jimmie Rodgers, star in the 1920s. Rodgers's memorable combination of African-American blues, cowboy yodeling, and Hawaiian guitar extended his influence far beyond the period of his short life. Rogie liked to mimic his odd guitar plucking and country vocals. He eventually recorded something of an ode to Rodgers called "Folk Blues" (later retitled "I Wish I Was a Cowboy").

Freetown in the fifties and sixties was a particularly good place for musicians. There were always parties to play for in the bustling capital, and a variety of bars competed for customers with the lure of live music. Recording, too, was becoming a means of generating both income and a measure of fame. European record companies had representatives roaming West Africa in search of talent; the British company Decca even had a mobile studio, which periodically visited Freetown.

Local entrepreneurs also sought a piece of the action. The most successful was a Nigerian named Jonathan Adenuga, who had

S. E. Rogie and Everetta Davies record a radio commercial in Freetown, Sierra Leone, circa 1964. Photo courtesy of S. E. Rogie

come to Freetown to attend Fourah Bay College (in those days the only institution of higher learning in West Africa) and stayed. In the early fifties, Adenuga decided to diversify his photography business and established a recording studio with a small monophonic Uher recorder and two microphones.[2] Known as Adenuga and Jonathan, publishing under the Nugatone label, the new venture was a boon to S. E. Rogie's budding career.

By 1952 Rogie had abandoned the tailoring profession, survived an acrimonious eleven months in the army, and settled in as a clerk-typist in Sierra Leone's accountant general's office. After work he continued to write and perform his songs for increasingly receptive audiences. "People were just telling me about the way my voice, it was good, they like my voice, say, 'Hey you could make records, you could make records,'" Rogie remembers. "And so somebody told me about a man who was there who was doing recording, the place where they were doing recording. So I went there, they listened to me, and they recorded my songs."

The year was 1955 or 1956—memories are clouded by the passage of time—and the man was Adenuga. He paid Rogie a flat fee of five pounds each for songs sung in the *Mende* language like "Jaimgbatutu," the story of a wise bird, and "Muhaleawai Mutihembeh, a song for the Sierra Leone People's Party, the dominant political organization of the time. Pressed in England into 78 RPM records, such early songs were usually Rogie singing with only his guitar or with a small chorus. Meanwhile, his growing reputation led to more lucrative work performing at parties. He supplemented that income by buying records wholesale from Adenuga and reselling them at a profit. Around the end of 1956 he was earning enough money to be able to quit his daytime job.

Radio also played a part in Rogie's musical ascendancy. Launched in 1934 as a rediffusion system feeding programs by wire to receiver-speakers in the homes of those who could afford it, the Sierra Leone Broadcasting Service (SLBS) converted to wireless transmission in 1955, making its programming available to a much wider audience. Rogie often made his way to Freetown's New England section and the SLBS studios—converted barracks that were home to Allied troops during World War II—to tell stories and sing songs for the country's expanding number of radio listeners.

In 1960, with the help of a wealthy patron, Rogie sent to England for his own tape recorder, a small one-track machine with inputs for two microphones. When inspiration struck, he set up the equipment at home. "I would wait when it's late at night, when it's quiet and no cars driving by and there was no noise outside. Then I would do my recording," he says. Afterward the tapes were sent off to a record manufacturer in England.

Recordings on the new Rogie label (later to become Rogiphone) were sometimes only Rogie and his guitar. At other times he employed musicians to provide vocal and rhythmic accompaniment. "These are musicians that are just hanging around me, you know," he explains. "If I need to do my recording, I train them, show them what to do, and they record with me and pay them something and that's the end of it. I might not even see some again."

Rogie record label from the 1960s

S. E. Rogie. Photo © 1986 Emmanuel Nado

Recording sessions often led to ingenious improvisation to achieve the desired effect. Bass sounds were sometimes created by a calabash—half of a hollowed-out gourd about the size and shape of a large mixing bowl—submerged upside down in a basin of water and beaten with the player's fist. Claves were occasionally modified by striking them against a table to produce a flatter, lower-pitched sound. A large wooden box became a bass drum.

After pressing, records were shipped back from England sport-ing a distinctive label in Sierra Leone's national colors, blue, white, and green. Rogie was emblazoned in bold black letters across the label's middle, the R and E equally large at either side, the O and I somewhat smaller, and the G in the center smaller still with the hole for the turntable spindle running through it.

Rogie's biggest record of the early days was the 1962 hit "My Lovely Elizabeth." "I just used the name Elizabeth, but the back-ground story was genuine," he says, recalling a real-life heartbreak. "It was based on my heaviest disappointment in my love affairs. A girl left me, I was disappointed, and I tried to express my feelings through that song. I just chose the name Elizabeth because I thought it would suit the song, and I liked it also." Recorded in the studios of SLBS, "Elizabeth" sold an estimated thirteen thousand copies in Sierra Leone[3] (an astonishing figure for the time given that record players were, for the most part, the property of more affluent city dwellers in a country whose population was largely rural) and thousands more when EMI picked it up for international distribution. But where a broken romance begot artistic success, Rogie's business relationship ended in dissolution. Suspicious of EMI's sales figures and disappointed in their royalty payments, he reverted to doing his own distribution.

As his popularity grew, Rogie began to perform and distribute records in the neighboring counties of Guinea and Liberia. He met with heads of state and lauded them in his music. Such praise sing-ing is an old tradition in many parts of Africa. Itinerant musicians often improvise songs in honor of local "big men" in hopes of being given a "dash" of money. Palm wine singers are no less eager for gain. Rogie extolled the virtues, real or imagined, of Liberian president Tubman, Guinea's Sekou Touré, President Houphouët-Boigny of Côte d'Ivoire, and several Sierra Leonean dignitaries at one time or another, both in live performance and on record. He recalls that on one occasion President Tubman rewarded him with one thousand dollars.[4]

In the midsixties Rogie put together a full-fledged band called the Morningstars. "It just came to me," he says. "The morning stars are bright, you know. I feel it's a lively music, it brightens people up, so I just decided to give it the name Morningstars." To his acoustic guitar he added an electric lead guitar and electric bass. His grab-bag collection of percussion instruments continued to supply the rhythm.

Along with Western instruments, Western sounds continued to influence African music. When Chubby Checker exploded in 1960 with his version of Hank Ballard's "The Twist," Africa could not escape the new craze. Rogie wrote several twist numbers for the new band, including "Awa Mutwistiga" and "Twist with the Morningstars," that were recorded around 1965. But these were only experimental pieces, he told writer Sarah Coxson. "That's not really my kind of music. That doesn't come from my soul. I really did that to try my hand at different sounds, not from a desire to do it. I wanted to prove how versatile I could be. With my talent I felt I could do anything outside African music. I didn't even like it at all, frankly."[5]

Songs with the new lineup that were more to his liking included "Baby Lef Marah" and "Man Stupid Being," commentaries on the behavior of the sexes recorded in Liberia with Liberian musicians who filled in when the real Morningstars were lured away by an unscrupulous promoter. The lead guitarists on those sessions was a talented player called Trouble Willie, so named, says Rogie, because wherever he played women always fought over him.

For Rogie, the sixties was a period of artistic accomplishment marred by personal excess. The old cliché "wine, women, and song" defined his life for most of the decade. Money came and went without heed; women and drink followed in much the same fashion. Twice, after disputes with musicians and promoters, he sold all his instruments to raise cash. The second time, in 1967, following his work in the sessions that produced "Baby Lef Marah" and three other equally strong numbers, Rogie decided to use the money to tour West Africa.

"I then left for the Ivory Coast [now officially named by its French translation, Côte d'Ivoire] full of hopes for the better," Rogie told writer Valerie Wilmer, "but I was terribly mistaken, for I found everything there completely different, especially that I had little knowledge of the French Language. By the end of three months I went completely out of cash. They drove me out of a hotel, seizing my typewriter, my Omega wrist watch as part payment of the hotel bill. I slept under a mango tree in a yard for 28 days, with no hope of getting any money just then."[6] With help from local residents who recognized him as the one who sang "My Lovely Elizabeth," a destitute Rogie wound up performing his paean to Houphouët-Boigny on Ivoirian television.

Earnings from the broadcast bought freedom for Rogie; he left for Ghana to visit Jerry Hansen of the Ramblers Dance Band. Hansen's highlife group had toured Sierra Leone in 1963, and the two had struck up an acquaintance. After his checkered experience with the Morningstars, Rogie hoped to learn from Hansen the mechanics of setting up a band and keeping it together. He moved on some weeks later for a look at the music scene in Nigeria, then backtracked west through what was then Dahomey (now Benin) and Togo, then north to Mali and Senegal before ending his nearly one-year trek back in Sierra Leone—penniless.

The journey had had its frustration and disappointment, but from a personal standpoint it was beneficial. Along the way Rogie began to explore his spirituality. He credits this awakening to a book called *The Art of Meditation* found on Jerry Hansen's bookshelf. The God he discovered in his reading began to change his life. With a newly developed sense of self-discipline, he abandoned his dangerously indulgent life-style and resumed his career.

1969 found Rogie recording again and performing a one-man "Self-Organized Folk and Cultural Exposition" at schools around the country. At the same time, he compiled the *Rogie International Song Book,* a collection of his work and some favorite songs from other artists. In the early seventies he served as an assistant director with the Sierra Leone National Dance Troupe and accompanied the group on a South American tour.

In 1973, hoping to conquer new territory, Rogie moved to the United States. "Back there [Sierra Leone] I was a big artist, and I had many American friends and fans who told me that if I came over here [America] I would become a millionaire overnight or make it fast," he says. "So I came here expressly to explore."

He settled in the San Francisco area, where, instead of millions, he found mostly disappointment mitigated by occasional success. Along with Irene Greene, an American friend and patron, he formed the R&G African Project, a small company designed to market his work and further the spread of African culture in America. He put together various bands of American musicians interested in learning to play African music, recorded two albums, and played uncountable numbers of live dates up and down the West Coast.

Perhaps his biggest accomplishment was an African cultural program he presented to schoolchildren and adults. A combination of music, lecture, and slides, the program, Rogie explains, helped "to clear up the myths about African cultures. I let them know that Africa has greatly contributed to the economic, social, and cultural prosperity of the world."

While his performances brought numerous proclamations and certificates of merit from local politicians, prosperity remained elusive. Rogie often found himself sweeping floors or delivering pizzas to earn enough money to live on. But circumstances began to change in 1986 when, at the urging of friends, he began to piece together some of his early recordings from surviving tapes haphazardly stored in a garage. Released as an album called *The 60s' Sounds of S. E. Rogie,* this compilation of raw, unadulterated palm wine music generated far more attention than Rogie's modern studio recordings.

Copies found their way to London and into the collection of influential BBC disc jockey Andy Kershaw. Kershaw not only pushed the music, he helped arrange a U.K. pressing of the record and a promotional tour for Rogie. The album was repackaged as *Palm Wine Guitar Music* by London's Cooking Vinyl label complete with new cover art and two additional tracks found in the collection of Wisconsin musicologist Naomi Ware. The promotional tour, a one-man show of story and song, generated such enthusiasm that Rogie decided to stay in England.

With an array of supporters unlike any he had ever seen—an established record company, a professional booking agency, enthusiastic radio promotion, and a well-disposed press—Rogie's career was reborn. Club dates were plentiful and performances critically acclaimed. He began to share billings with more mainstream stars like Billy Bragg and Jonathan Richman. WOMAD signed him for their 1989 festivals, and bookings rolled in from the Netherlands, Germany, France, and Italy.

Nevertheless, there were occasional instances of mild disenchantment. During a break from performances in Italy, the sight of the Vatican's lavish display of riches caused Rogie, son of an impoverished nation, to rethink his Christianity. In business matters, the persistent problem of reconciling an artist's expectations with record company accounts of sales and royalties surfaced in a dispute with Cooking Vinyl. The issue led him to sign with the rival Workers Playtime label for two new albums, *The Palm Wine Sounds of S. E. Rogie* and *The New Sounds of S. E. Rogie,* the latter recorded with a newly formed band he calls his Palm Wine Tappers.

To purge any feelings of disappointment, Rogie has only to recall the darkest hours of his West African pilgrimage or his discouraging American sojourn. England has delivered him from such distress. For this African musician, the struggle to prosper in the West has had a happy ending.

A Vanishing Breed

Big Fayia

6

Recording artists in Sierra Leone were a vanishing breed in the 1980s, victims of the country's economic collapse and a massive influx of tape cassettes and recording machines that produced a tidal wave of music piracy. With the tools of their trade nearly unobtainable, and profits from their work vanishing into the pockets of others, many of Sierra Leone's musicians stopped recording; many others have pursued their careers abroad. One who perseveres in Freetown, resolutely resisting the trend, is Mustapha Sahr Fayia, known to the music world as Big Fayia.

He built his following in the sixties on a foundation of clever lyrics sung in Mende and Krio, the country's pidgin English lingua franca, coupled with a gift for devising infectious, endearing melodies. Beginning with his own five-piece combo, later with the Military Dance Band, and currently as leader of a troupe of traditional performers, Fayia's career has spanned the heyday and the hell of Sierra Leone's music industry.

Between performances of his West Africa Mask Dancers at local tourist spots and travels abroad for recording, Big Fayia can usually be found at "bottom mango," the last *poda poda* (minibus) stop near the main gate to Wilberforce Army Barracks. There, atop a towering hill overlooking Freetown, he maintains a small kiosk—the word *Maryland* splashed across its front—where friends from his twenty years in the army pause for conversation and a cold pint of beer. Income from the kiosk supplements the uncertain rewards of a musical career and helps provide support for his wife and six children.

Fayia's ancestral home is the town of Dia in the Kailahun District of eastern Sierra Leone, but he spent most of his youth in the Southern Province city of Bo. Nothing in his early years, in the late

53

Big Fayia in the early 1970s. Photo courtesy of Sasu Adjivon

forties and early fifties, seemed to portend a musical career. He lived a normal schoolboy life with the aim of becoming a mechanical engineer. But after finishing his studies at Bo's United Christian Council Secondary School, Fayia could find no opportunity to pursue engineering. In need of a job, he answered an advertisement for employment with the Prisons Department and was hired in 1957.

In the island community of Bonthe, Fayia's first prison post, he discovered his latent musical talent in the company of a local palm wine musician named Pa Cooper. "That was the very first time I saw somebody playing guitar," he recalls. "I was hearing the Zulus [Sierra Leone's generic term for music from South Africa] and this man, S. E. Rogers. I used to hear his records by then, but I don't know him, and I had never seen anybody playing guitar. That was the very first time, so straightaway I was interested."[1] He paid Pa Cooper for a lesson and soon bought his own guitar.

Compared to recent times, the fifties and sixties were decades of prosperity in Sierra Leone. European trading companies Paterson-Zochonis, United Africa Company, Kingsway, and Compagnie Française d'Afrique Occidentale, along with local businessmen like the Lebanese Bahsoon Brothers, imported a wide array of consumer goods including radios, record players, records, and musical instruments. "It's not like now, we don't have guitars around," says Fayia. "But PZ was having guitar, UAC and then CFAO, French company, and everybody was having guitar."

As he learned to play, Fayia hung out with other musicians to pick up what knowledge he could. But the stigma attached to the music profession soon made him the subject of gossip. "I don't drink. I don't smoke. I don't chew kola," he explains. "So people started saying, 'Ah! I think Fayia wanted to drink now, because he started playing guitar.'"

Over the next few years he was transferred to various prison posts around the country, continuing all the while to play music. His skill improved to the point where he could travel "in a launch without paying because of my guitar, in a train without paying because of my guitar." Eventually he was posted to Freetown, where his musical career began to take off.

In 1963 he formed a five-piece band called the Blue Diamonds, employing three guitars, conga, and drum, and cut a record for Freetown's leading producer, Jonathan Adenuga, called "Garri Go

Gi Yu Beleh" (a double-entendre: Garri, food made from ground
cassava, "will give you a belly" or "make you pregnant"). When the
band played a dance at Marampa Mines seventy-five miles east of
Freetown, the performance so impressed managers at Delco, the
mine's operator in those days, that they invited Fayia and his musicians to make the mining town their home base. "They were paying
me, the prisons, ten pounds a month. So Delco said we'll give you
thirteen pounds, so I had to leave [the prison post]," he says. The
band played in the Lunsar/Marampa area for nearly a year under
the name Iron Ore Jazz.

In 1965 the army's parade band came to Marampa to play for
Delco's annual long-service award ceremony. The soldiers, who
had heard the hot sounds of Iron Ore Jazz, began to talk to Fayia
about forming a military dance band. "They convinced me to come
to the army," he says. "And I left Delco, came [to Freetown] to the
army to come and make the first dance band."

Competition among Freetown bands was fierce in the 1960s.
There were several outstanding groups including Akpata Jazz
(sponsored by Prime Minister Albert Margai), Geraldo Pino's
Heartbeats, the Ticklers, Red Stars, Eddie and his West Africans (a
mixed band of Liberians and Sierra Leoneans), and Ry-co Jazz
from the Congo (Zaire). Fayia joined the competition with his
Sierra Leone Military Dance Band.

"When I went there, they gave me the uniform, and then [made
me] undergo the necessary training as other soldiers," he remembers. "I told them that they should employ my men, because I'll not
be able to train soldiers just for one or two months to be able to
play. So they employed all my men; then we were training another
soldiers now to become musicians at that time." Advertised as the
Military Dance Band headed by Famous Fayiah, it featured the
three guitars, conga, and drum of the old Iron Ore Jazz along with
a new horn section of saxophone, trombone, and trumpets. Under
Fayia's direction the band built a reputation as a tight and versatile
group that could play "copyright" and original music with the
same relish.

But Fayia was not completely satisfied. Around 1968 or 1969,
seeing that there was money to be made apart from his army salary,
he began to record songs with a session band called the Invissible

[*sic*] Five. Since military officers generally knew him as Mustapha or M.S., he used the name Big Fayia to conceal his involvement. The Invissible Five included guitarists Stanley Kabia and the late Kangajue, conga player Abu Sillah, Sillah's brother Mohammed (known as Crappy Johnnie), and at various times singers Hakim Janneh (Jannesco) and Abou Whyte.

Nearly everyone involved, including Fayia, takes credit for organizing the Invissible Five, but the most plausible recollection comes from Sierra Leone Broadcasting Service producer Chris During. "My idea was that the Invissible Five should be strictly a recording band and a support, an accompanying band, for artists that cannot [afford] a band," During explains. "And when we record I can get this band to support. In case recording needed other instruments, I can commission people who played those instruments to join the Five. When Fayia came into it, he took me as his recording manager, and I placed this band at his disposal. In a thing like that, I would say Big Fayia and the Invissible Five on the label."[2]

During presided over scores of recording sessions at the SLBS studios, producing, in addition to Big Fayia and the Invissible Five, most of the top groups in Sierra Leone, including S. E. Rogie, the Heartbeats, Super Combo, Salia Koroma, and Ebenezer Calender. Much of the recording was done "unbeknown to the authorities," says During, often coordinated with a group's appearance for a radio band show. The radio shows would be taped for broadcast, then the session would continue with songs recorded for disc.

Studio One at SLBS—today largely inoperable—is spacious, perhaps twenty by thirty feet, with a ceiling nearly twenty feet high. In the center of one wall is a glass partition and doorway leading to the control room, which in the sixties and seventies housed a full-track recorder and a mixing board capable of accepting eight inputs.

To help achieve the desired mix, During would separate the musicians with movable baffles. "Like the vocalist, I would separate him with wooden curtains from the rest of the band," he says. "Like the percussion section, they tend to [play loud]. . . . The vibration of some instruments reverbs around, those types of instruments. . . . I had to screen it from the rest." If a band was large and more than eight microphones were needed, During improvised to increase the mixing board's capacity. "Like for the percussion section, I'll use the junction box where I put more than one microphone to one channel. . . . So if they're properly rehearsed, like the tambourine, the conga, and the drums, . . . they balance themselves."

Rehearsals were important to get musicians used to the demands of recording. During explains that "it's very difficult [for musicians] to adapt themselves to studio conditions. Seeing that the African, they've been used to acoustic instruments, they have [had] to force themselves to play loud. Even when I have electrical instruments for them, they want to burst their tops off. You have to bring them down to that [studio] condition."

Completed tapes that were not expressly commissioned were sold to one of the growing number of Freetown record labels like Adenuga's Nugatone, A-Z, J. T. Stores, or Bassophone. Big Fayia and the Invissible Five produced a string of hit records in this manner, including "Before E Burn Make E Wet" (a title with vaguely lewd connotations, literally "before he burns, make him wet"), "New Love No No Ben Mot" (new love doesn't know lies), and "Watin Make Baby Day Cry" (what makes baby cry). Several other recordings During calls "clandestine," done "unbeknown to me," were issued as Big Fayia and the Invissible Four.

In the early seventies, through what he believes were petty jealousies and politics, Fayia was relieved of his position as leader of the Military Dance Band and transferred to the army's regimental concert band, where for several years he played marches and classical music on the saxophone. In 1975 Blackpool, a powerful Freetown football (soccer) team, held a contest to find a theme song. Fayia claimed first prize, a trip to London to record his composition. The following year he went back to England, this time sponsored by the army, to study classical music.

In London he met Sierra Leonean producers Akie Deen and J. F. Samuh and recorded for each of them at different times. Deen had some music tracks recorded by a Sierra Leonean band called Sabanoh 75. Fayia overdubbed lyrics he composed to produce the hit "Alay Wu Waa." Recordings done for Samuh were Fayia's compositions with backing from African musicians living in London.

Great songs came out of those sessions, including "Want Want No Get," "Me Back (Jealous Woman, Jealous Man)," and "Respect."

On his return to Sierra Leone in 1976, Fayia was transferred back to the Military Dance Band, and the group embarked on a series of goodwill tours sponsored by the All People's Congress government of President Siaka Stevens. On separate occasions the band toured Nigeria, Liberia, Gambia, the USSR, Hungary, and Cuba. Fayia remembers audience reaction varied widely. In the USSR and Hungary "they used to listen [to the music] really carefully. Even if it was raining they used to stand there and listen to it. And in fact some used to dance, [but] the Cubans, they dance. When we play they dance because they are Africans."

The Havana trip in 1978 came out of an invitation to a music festival. "We competed with twenty-five bands, and I come first," Fayia recalls. "The band which I was fearing was. . . Keletigui from Guinea and Bantous [de la] Capitale from Congo. But when Keletigui came, I knock out Keletigui. So it remained the Bantous Capitale from Congo. They were twenty-two. When those boys started playing, I said, 'Oh! Well this, I have no choice. I think they are going to beat me anyway.' But after they played, because they played the same rhythm, the same music, so I called my men immediately. We come to do a meeting, I say, 'Well now, we are going to play variety, because we are good in copyright. People call us musicians, but now I am going to call us magicians.' Because while we are here we play music from Ghana, from Guinea, from Ivory Coast, from Nigeria, from where we come from, and all over the world."

Following their Havana triumph, Fayia and the Military Dance Band went on to make their first and only recordings, which included an album in honor of the 1980 Organization of African Unity conference that was held in Freetown. In 1985, after twenty years of military service as his country's musical ambassador, Big Fayia left the relative comfort of the army to pursue his career in the bleakness of Freetown's devastated music scene.

Throughout the 1980s Sierra Leone's economy lurched relentlessly into depression. Foreign exchange, necessary to import instruments and studio equipment, all but dried up as prices for the country's produce declined on world markets, its wealth of gold and diamonds disappeared across porous borders, and corrupt officials looted the dwindling treasury.

If economic ruin was an agent of death, record pirates were executioners. "When you make a record," Fayia explains, "they buy only one, start cassetting them. And record has about three or four songs, but cassette has about five here, five there. . . . Then bands cannot make record any more, because they can't sell." As a result of these twin afflictions, many musicians left the profession or moved abroad. All the recording studios folded.

But Fayia refuses to give up on the music business. In 1987, with help from Sierra Leone's president Joseph Momoh, Big Fayia and a new band called Jehpeh-Londo, featuring singers Abou Whyte and Dr. Chessie and veteran guitarist Bankole Gabba, traveled to Côte D'lvoire to record a new album. The lead track, set to a rock-solid reggae beat, urges farmers to produce more food and exhorts the nation's unemployed to return to the farm. Called "Farmers," the song was a key component in President Momoh's effort to rally the country behind his Green Revolution Program.

But the ten-song album, entitled simply *Big Fayia,* is more than an exercise in propaganda. It contains much clever social commentary sung in the sharp, witty style that is Fayia's trademark. "Snuff Chick," for example, tells a humorous tale of a girl who doesn't kiss because she eats snuff, and "Etara Layn" sings the praises of Big Fayia himself. In a partially successful attempt to discourage piracy, the album was released on cassette tape in collaboration with Freetown's main taping parlors.

Perhaps even more creative than his alliance with record pirates is his use of traditional music and dance. With the implements of popular music scarce or nonexistent, Fayia decided to form a troupe of artists who could equip themselves without regard to the vagaries of international economics. Big Fayia's West Africa Mask Dancers are a twenty-member entourage of dancers clothed in the marvelously extravagant costumes of traditional "devils" and percussion players extracting the scintillating rhythms of rural villages from instruments created by local artisans. The troupe dazzles foreign tourists who flock in increasing numbers to luxurious hotels along Sierra Leone's breathtaking beaches.

Fayia hopes that in time his dance troupe will generate enough income so that money can be set aside to purchase equipment for a new pop band. "It is now that I've started," he declares, "Because I am waiting for my children [who are budding musicians]. And they are trying; they are coming up." Meanwhile he is content to use local materials as instruments of creativity while he strives to hasten the day when Sierra Leone's flagging music industry will revive.

Graceland's Heartbeat

Francis Fuster

7

"It came to me like in a dream, because as I was sitting home the phone rang. They say this is a call from America. 'You wanna play the Graceland Paul Simon gig?' I went blank. I didn't remember who Paul Simon was." More than two years after that call, Sierra Leone's Francis Fuster still speaks of it in tones of wonder and amazement. "I—I mean, how did he know me?"[1]

Hugh Masekela was the likely source. His presence, along with that of Miriam Makeba, conferred a special mantle of authenticity on the Graceland tour, and Fuster had earned his musical reputation as the South African trumpeter's percussionist. Their association dates back to a 1974 recording session in Nigeria when Fuster was still with his own band, Baranta, successor to Sierra Leone's seminal pop group the Heartbeats.

Relaxed in his comfortable northeast London townhouse—purchased in part with a share of the Graceland bonanza—Fuster looks for all the world like the distant cousin of a Mexican revolutionary. Dark eyes punctuate his thin, fair-skinned face. His bushy afro is scooped out in the middle as if parted by a burst of machine-gun fire.

Beneath the distinctive hairdo resides an acute sense of rhythm sharpened during childhood. Fuster grew up in a central area of Freetown known as Kru Town. His mother was a singer, and his father and grandfather, although seamen by profession, were excellent amateur musicians. Traditionally Kru people are seafarers, so Kru Town was a natural meeting point for African and Western culture. "When anything comes into an African city," he says, "It usually comes through the bays. So even the music came through the bays at that time." His seafaring father would bring home records by Louis Jordan, Nat King Cole, and Ella Fitzgerald, while the streets shook to the beat of traditional dancers and drummers.

Fuster admired the drummers. "It was a manly thing to me," he recalls. "It was very muscular. These guys were strong guys, and I admired their attack on the drums." One man in particular, Batu Biosei, caught his fancy, and the ten-year-old Fuster begged him for lessons. "I would go straight to his house from school. . . . And I would do all the chores. And then we would sit down and just play for a couple of hours. The love of drums happened at that time. And since that time I don't remember wanting to do anything else."

Soon after it had begun, his apprenticeship was cut short by Biosei's untimely death. But the setback was only temporary, for one day Fuster's mother took him to Freetown's Church of the Lord Aladura. The sound of celebratory drumbeats cascaded into the street as he approached the building, and he was hooked. For the next four years he played drums in the church's daily services. "Most of my drumming, what happens now, today, actually took form in that church," he declares. "Batu gave me like what you would call a greening. But the first time something came out of my soul was when I entered the church. I could construct rhythmic patterns before I knew about what I was doing."

In 1962, a few months into his second year at Fourah Bay College, Fuster left school following an altercation with a lecturer. To pass time he put together a dance team called Kompara Jazz, which entertained at parties to the accompaniment of the day's hit records. One such performance at a graduation dance led to Fuster's encounter with the Heartbeats.

The Heartbeats, the dance's main attraction, was essentially a West African rock band that specialized in playing cover versions of Western hits from the likes of Cliff Richard and the Shadows. The band's drummer failed to show up, so although he had no experience with Western-style kit drums, Fuster volunteered to sit in. "The experience! The excitement! The applause! I mean I got applause as a dancer, but sitting there and actually playing music and people liking it and standing up, affected me too much."

The band had formed in 1961 with singer Gerald Pine, guitarist Balogun "Dynamite" Johnson-Williams, and drummer Reuben

Williams. Bassist George Keister and Hassan Deen, whose specialty was Congolese-style vocals, were soon added to the mix, and out of concern over their drummer's erratic behavior, the players replaced him with Fuster.

The 1960s was a decade of prosperity for bands in Sierra Leone after the epoch of portable sound systems, known locally as "amplifiers," had created a temporary lull in demand for live music. Following the march of Western technology, windup gramophones and fragile 78 RPM records gave way to more durable 45s and electrified record players that could be connected to larger amplifiers and speakers. Rock and roll sounds of Elvis Presley, Cliff Richard, and Tommy Steele began to overshadow the music of local groups. Producer Chris During recalls, "When these records started coming in and discotheques started building up, people started hiring these amplifiers. . . . Before then even [for] house parties people used to hire bands. But with the advent of these amplifiers, house parties no more needed bands."[2]

Credit for the renaissance of live music belongs, in part, to a touring Congolese (Zairean) band called Ry-co Jazz. "When that band came it made such an impact on the young people," says During. "When the Ry-co Jazz came, oh! It swept the young people off their feet." Ry-co Jazz, a trio consisting of guitar, saxophone, and conga, which became a quartet with the addition of a bass player in Freetown, created fresh excitement with their flashy, stylish presentation and engaging mixture of Latin and Congolese rhythms.

One of those smitten was the Heartbeats' leader, Gerald Pine. Pine had been juggling work in his radio repair shop with the demands of rehearsing his new band without much success. Music occupied increasing amounts of his time, much to the annoyance of customers who wanted their radios repaired as promised. Music, especially the Latin fascination, won out. Pine changed his name to Geraldo Pino, and the band was billed as Geraldo Pino and his Heartbeats.

The group played mostly "copyright" music in live performance. Recordings on the Pino record label were Latin-sounding original compositions like "Maria Lef for Waka" and "Oh Ye Charanga" (described on the label as Spanish, although Naomi Ware points out that it "is a nonsense lyric consisting of 'words' that sound like Spanish but are not and mean nothing".)[3] They

Francis Fuster (*left*) and Geraldo Pino in Nigeria, 1970. Photo courtesy of Francis Fuster

staged dances and packed Freetown nightclubs like the Tiwana, Flamingo, and Palm Beach Club. Heartbeats skipped for a moment in late 1963 when the band was involved in a serious road accident. Both Fuster and George Keister were hospitalized but eventually recovered.

When the punchy new music of Memphis and Motown began to cross the Atlantic, the Heartbeats added soul to their repertoire. By the midsixties the band was traveling regularly to Liberia, Ghana, and Nigeria playing tight covers of American soul songs. Propelled by Fuster's devastating drums and Pino's James Brown dips and struts, they fomented West Africa's soul craze. In Ghana, groups like the El Pollos and the Barbecues sought to capitalize on the new sound's mushrooming popularity. In Nigeria it was the same story with Segun Bucknor and his Soul Assembly, the Hykkers, and the Clusters led by Joni Haastrup.

No less a personage than Fela Anikulapo-Kuti was bedazzled by the Heartbeats when they stormed into Nigeria in 1966. "They were great, I must be frank with you," says Fela. "They copied James Brown throughin, throughout, every note, every style. And they had the equipment. See they brought this new equipment which nobody had ever had before. You know this clean five microphones, different channel equipment. Before they came into my country bands only used one microphone, at the time, a whole band. But they came in with five microphones, and the sound, and it's deep, you know. . . . So nobody wanted to hear anybody but the Heartbeats. So they drove everybody out of the market."[4]

Despite occasional personnel changes—Dynamite, for one, left to form his own band—the group prospered. As the soul craze wore off, the players weaned themselves from covering Western pop songs by developing original material. "When that started to happen," says Fuster, "the best writers got stronger in the band. [Guitarist] Arnold Nylander became very strong because he understood his music and could explain it. So he became like a musical director of the band. And he and I wrote most of the stuff that we played."

Francis Fuster

Francis Fuster (wearing headband) and Okyerema Asante on tour with Paul Simon's Graceland troupe. Photo: Harrison Funk. Copyright © 1987 Paul Simon. Used by permission of the owner

By 1972 tension within the group was high. Pino's handling of money and management had become a constant source of friction. "We were all putting everything [in] to take it to Sierra Leone to build studios, to expand record companies," says Fuster. "We were gonna do big things. We had big plans. And the guy [Pino] went crazy with the money, because he had total control of it." After playing some Christmas dates in Ghana, Fuster quit and went to Lagos. Most of the others soon followed, leaving Pino odd man out. The Fuster faction resumed playing under the name Baranta, a Krio word that means "rebel."

In 1974 Fuster met Hugh Masekela through his friend Liberian singer Miatta Fahnbulleh—a meeting that led to an album project with Masekela, Fahnbulleh, and Baranta recording together in Lagos. Incredibly, the music was lost when the master tape was inadvertently left on a train in Nigeria. Nevertheless, working with Masekela and producer Stewart Levine was a revelation for Fuster. He heard sounds he had previously only imagined. The music "came for the first time alive to me," he says. "It had breath. You know? It had pulse."

Baranta broke up in 1976 when Fuster got stranded in New York, where he had gone in search of better equipment and performance techniques. He finally scraped together enough money to get back to Freetown in 1978. There he taught karate—he had achieved a black belt while in New York—and booked entertainment for the newly opened Bintumani Hotel. He also staged shows at the City Hall auditorium that featured various performers and his own satirical monologues.

Fuster's bitingly humorous social critiques generated such political heat that by 1982 he felt he had to leave the country. He moved to London where, once again by chance, he encountered Masekela and quickly accepted his offer of a job. Settling in next to the band's kit drummer, he began developing his unique percussion array, which has come to include an assortment of hand drums, timbales, and cymbals. Whenever Fuster plays with Masekela's band, sparkling interplay between the drummers is a highlight of each performance. "I've always loved working with Masekela," he declares. "I think he's one of the few African guys that really know what's happening within the international music scenes."

Their association paid interest when Fuster was invited to join Paul Simon's 1987 Graceland tour. "That's the biggest thing I've ever done," he says, still seemingly in awe. "For an African boy coming from my direction, it was big for me. . . . I was so unsure of myself. I was so uncertain. When I went for the rehearsals it was, for me, it was a big audition. It was amazing. But it was a good feeling that I could do it, that I could play at that level."

Paul Simon's *Graceland* album was one of the finest American pop records of the eighties. More surprising than its groundbreaking use of the closely linked rhythms of South Africa, southwest Louisiana, and the Texas-Mexico border was its overwhelming popular acceptance. *Graceland* was both an artistic and financial success despite having the temerity to challenge the record establishment's Top Forty formula.

Simon's Graceland troupe, featuring Hugh Masekela and Miriam Makeba with the duo of Fuster and Hedzoleh Soundz alumnus Okyerema Asante on percussion, opened with three concerts in the Netherlands and Germany before its tumultuous, cathartic appearance in Zimbabwe. Fuster revels in his recollection of the experience. "You know what it means to me to walk in a hall, to walk in a stadium, and it's sold out? For me? First big tour. Sold out seventy-four [concerts]. Australia, America, Africa, British Isles, Europe. It was good for me. I was lucky. But I'm pleased to say that all of that just showed me that I had potential myself to go higher than that or as high by myself. So from this point on I'm going all the way. I'm going to die trying."

These days, in spare moments between tour and recording dates with Masekela and free-lance session work, Fuster is putting the finishing touches on his first solo album, *Imagination*. He calls it a work of love. "When there's love, political issues are easy to solve. But where there's greed and hate, it's difficult to put your music across. But if we can talk about love and equality and honesty, maybe it will help."

Fuster wrote most of the songs and, in addition to drumming, plays some guitar and sings for the first time since the days of Baranta. "I like to think of it as music for the soul," he says. "I feel some responsibility towards my people. And I need to help them with my music if that's the only way I can. . . . And doing that to me at this time seems to be very important."

Dance the Highlife

8

Nana Ampadu

It's almost as if Michael Jackson were appearing in the crowded hotel ballroom. The flash of a hundred cameras lights the room like fireworks. A thousand voices squeal with deafening shrillness. The African Brothers International band has already warmed up the largely African audience in suburban Washington, D.C. Now it's leader, Nana Kwame Ampadu I, makes his regal entrance. Short and slender, almost boyish in appearance, he wades through the crowd on the way to the bandstand gesturing like an African pope blessing his flock. Like Jackson, Ampadu is a show business veteran. The youthful looks belie his forty-five years, nearly thirty of which have been spent as a popular highlife guitarist in the West African country of Ghana.

As the packed house amply demonstrates, highlife is enjoying a renaissance. A popular style of African music for more than three decades beginning in the 1930s, highlife was suddenly swept aside in the midsixties by the explosion of Congo music and an avalanche of sounds from British and American pop groups. Now, with African music capturing an increasing share of the international market, highlife is being discovered by new generations both inside and outside the continent.

Highlife music evolved in the British colonies along the West African coast. The colonies were musical melting pots of rhythms and melodies of the indigenous people, piano and hymn music of Christian missionaries, brass band and fife and drum music of military garrisons, and other sounds of Europe and the Americas arriving via radio and records.

While highlife has roots all along the West African coast, the Gold Coast (now Ghana) is widely credited as its birthplace. Located on the Gulf of Guinea, it was a major port of call for slave ships sailing the Atlantic waters. Ancient castles, where captured Africans were imprisoned before shipment to Europe and America, still dot the shoreline in places like Elmina and Cape Coast. Following slavery's abolition, merchant ships brought manufactured goods to trade for gold and cocoa, while in spare moments their sailors exchanged folk songs and sea shanties with the local people.

With the advent of the world wars, Europe's African colonies became staging areas for Allied troops and fertile recruiting grounds for the enlistment of Africans to help fight in Europe and the Far East. In the Gold Coast's capital, Accra, saloons like the Roger Club, European Club, and later the Bashoun and Metropole sprang up featuring local bands playing a variety of music, especially highlife.

"'The term highlife,'" Yebuah Mensah (brother of the "king" of dance-band highlife, E. T. Mensah) explained to musicologist John Collins, "'was created by people who gathered around the dancing clubs. . . . The people outside called it the highlife as they did not reach the class of the couples going inside, who not only had to pay a relatively high entrance fee of about 7s [shillings] 6d [pence]; but also had to wear full evening dress, including top-hats if they could afford it.'"[1]

Two dominant strains of highlife emerged. Dance-band highlife featured sweet-sounding horns in a lineup similar to an American jazz combo. The players infused Western music with African touches to entertain their colonial occupiers and a burgeoning black elite. The relatively staid rags, waltzes, and fox-trots of the West were transformed in this African milieu of polyrhythms and traditional melodies into a fresh, spirited style more attuned to the African concept of music as a functional, participatory element of society.

Guitar-band highlife, the second strain, took something of an opposite path. African musicians borrowed the most appealing elements of foreign styles and incorporated them into their own works aimed at urban working-class and rural audiences. Songs that were played on local instruments like thumb piano (*apremprensemma* or, if you like, *aprempremsewa*) and Akan lute (*seprewa*) were easily adaptable to the Western-style guitar.[2]

Beginning in the early sixties, Nana Ampadu parlayed his self-taught guitar skills and flair for musical composition into a career as one of the leading players of the guitar-band style of highlife. His African Brothers band has grown from a small group of about five or six members, when it was founded in 1963, into a troupe of nearly two dozen. On the strength of its live performances and recorded output of more than fifty albums and a hundred singles, the band is one of Ghana's top attractions. *Nana* is, in fact, an honorary title meaning "king," which Ampadu won in 1972 by placing first in the National Guitar Band Competition.

Ampadu started out as a singer, a talent he developed while in school in the 1950s. Born in the town of Obo in Kwahu District in eastern Ghana, he refined his musical ear by listening to radio and records. He remembers hearing British guitarist Tommy Steele and Nigerians Victor Uwaifo and Rex Lawson, along with Otis Redding and Pat Boone, but his favorite performer was the great Ghanaian guitarist, E. K. Nyame. "When we were young, we were many in our house, the children, and each of us had his idol band, and my idol band was E. K. Nyame," he says. "So during 'Listeners' Choice' . . . we had a bet on our food and our meat. Whoever's band records were played more on the radio, it means you win. So I was always with E. K.'s band."[3]

With his school days over and a disappointing job search in Accra behind him, Ampadu found work with the Ministry of Agriculture back in his home district and began to write songs in his spare time. He became encouraged, he says, when he gave several of the compositions to Jerry Hansen, leader of the Ramblers Dance Band, "and all of them were hit numbers."

Stirred by these first glimmers of hope for a musical career, Ampadu returned to Accra in 1960. There, with the help of a relative, he was hired as a singer by bandleader P. K. Yamoah. It was a short-lived gig, however, for Yamoah, who like most musicians of the era held a daytime job, was soon transferred to another city.

Ampadu stayed in Accra, found work with "a drugstore firm," and bought a guitar with his earnings. Another musician taught him the finger positions, and the rest he picked up from a book and intensive practice. In 1962 he caught on with a band called T.O. Jazz (named for its leader, T. O. Ampoma), but again only as a singer. "When I was with T. O. I was very good on the guitar," he recalls. "But in those days . . . most of the bands were playing only one guitar at bandstand, and so it was very difficult for, you see, just a mere bandsman to be given the guitar to play."

Fearing he would never get a decent chance with an established group, Ampadu and some friends took on the formidable challenge of creating their own band. Family disapproval, he says, made the task particularly difficult: "In those days whenever you talk of be-

DMS Communication Design / San Francisco

coming a musician it's some sort of taboo in your family, because
they say [musicians] meddle with the moral life, like drinking,
chasing women, and other [things]. So nobody's parents or rela-
tives wanted their child to be a musician." But one of the group,
Eddie Donkor, had an uncle (there's a rich uncle in every culture)
with some instruments the budding musicians could use, so in
1963 the African Brothers band was born.

The group broke in slowly, playing dances and weddings while
continuing to work their individual day jobs. But to build a band's
stature and reputation, making records was essential. The African
Brothers got their recording break in 1966 from Philips West
Africa Limited. Grouped around a single microphone in Philips's
rudimentary Accra studio, the players recorded a single called
"Agyanka Dabere" using guitar, upright string bass, congas, and
vocals.

"When the recording of music started, most of our musicians
sung about death," Ampadu says. "Because in those days we were
very particular with mourning. You see, mourning became a part of
our [musicians'] problem, you see, it became a part of our service to
our family and to ourselves. So we thought of . . . a song about
mourning, about the orphan. That's why I made that 'Agyanka
Dabere,' you see. It's about death, that you lose your father and
who is going to take care of you and all that. But as time went on
you would be coming in with one or two of love song and then
story songs, proverbial songs and all that."

The African Brothers scored their first big hit the following year
with "Ebi Tie Ye" sung in the Twi language. "It was a very sensational record," says Ampadu. "In fact I had composed a lot of songs
which were very popular, but because of the essence, because of the
title of this song, you see, the title made it popular. 'Ebi Tie Ye,'
'some are living well and others are living very poorly,' or 'some are
rich, others are too poor.'"

Like many of Ampadu's compositions, "Ebi Tie Ye" tells a story
through the skillful use of metaphor. It describes how an antelope
successfully forces adjournment of a meeting of animals because he
is being denied full participation by a bullying leopard. "Ok-
waduo," another song of the same vintage that tells the story of a
wild ox who tricks a hunter into releasing him, thus ensuring more
severe treatment for the next to be caught, was widely believed to

Nana Ampadu

be about the members of the Nkrumah government, which had recently been overthrown.[4] "Few of them were political," Ampadu
slyly explains. "But I just wouldn't say directly political, but the listeners would just refer to an incident that happened in the country
and say, 'Look, you think this musician sang this song about this
case?' But maybe that is not the real motive behind the composition."

One of the group's best numbers is a love song of sadness.
"Awerehow" tells of lovers who take their relationship for granted
until one day they are separated and realize how much they miss
each other. It is a beautiful example of the richness of the African
Brothers' brand of highlife. Lush, tight vocal harmonies sail across
an undulating sea of interweaving guitars and percussion. The song
has proven durable enough to be recycled in a reggae version.

Ampadu works out new songs on the guitar or sometimes by
just singing. "You see," he explains, "with my music, I think the

whole thing begins from talent. Because at many a time I wouldn't be thinking of anything, and then a tune will just come into my mind. And simultaneously, when I get a tune, I will get some words to move along with it. So immediately I feel this thing, I just go [get] a tape recorder and record it so that later on I rewrite it and compose it." When rehearsing, he often solicits ideas from the other players to flesh out a new song. Ampadu calls his sound "Af-rihili," a combination of the words *African* and *highlife,* but he has experimented with other styles and even invented a short-lived fusion of highlife and afro-beat called "locomotive."

When working back home in Ghana, the African Brothers band includes a number of actors and becomes a "concert party." An African descendant of vaudeville, the concert party is a Ghanaian tradition dating to the 1920s. Largely male troupes travel around the country entertaining audiences with highlife songs and a variety of plays. Short humorous skits and a longer moralistic feature presentation are performed by the actors who, depending on the situation, might appear in exaggerated, minstrel-style makeup or dressed as women. Many of Ghana's guitar bands have adopted the concert party as a way of bolstering their popularity and earning more money.[5]

John Miller Chernoff tells of an African Brothers' production in which "the villain becomes jealous when a friend goes hunting and encounters dwarfs who reward him for his courtesy with a bag of gold." Although the friend shares his windfall with him, the villain goes to get more for himself. Despite his rudeness, the dwarfs give him a bag of gold with a warning to keep the bag closed until he arrives home. Fearing he may have to share his gift, the villain attempts to remove the gold before reaching his village. "Unfortunately, when he puts his hand into the bag, he discovers that he cannot remove it again. Shouting for help, he returns home. The medicine man cannot treat the dwarfs' magic, and in the end the villain must amputate his hand in order to free himself."[6]

Nana Ampadu and his fellow musicians would do well to find the dwarfs with bags of gold, because, just as it happened in Zaire and Sierra Leone, the deadly combination of economic decline and evolving technology has devastated Ghana's music industry. The continuing devaluation of Ghanaian currency and scarcity of for-

eign exchange make it nearly impossible to purchase imported instruments and recording equipment. There are a few studios in
Accra and to the north in Kumasi, but none is first-rate, and all are
often booked for months in advance. When he can find a conve-
nient opening, Ampadu records in the studios of the Ghana Film
Corporation, but increasingly he and his fellow musicians travel
abroad to record. Many have left Ghana permanently. "I think," he
says, "it's because of the inputs, the gadgets. In Europe and in
America we have many sophisticated gadgets whereby we want to
make the music very [presentable], and we decide recording in
those countries for more, you know, improvement in the recording
system."

Once the music is on tape, getting it pressed into records is another hurdle. Ampadu estimates that Ghana's two pressing plants
operate at only 25 percent of capacity at most, and the quality of
their pressings is poor. Since the early eighties he has chosen to
send his tapes to Europe or America to be made into records, which
are then distributed abroad and imported for sale at home. The
rapid acceptance of the compact disc in Western markets poses an
additional dilemma. Does one aim at the overseas market and invest scarce capital in a compact disc release or concentrate instead
on the home front where records and tapes are still favored?

Despite the compact disc's intrusion, for Ghanaian musicians
the cassette tape has, more than any other format, caused the biggest headache. Since about the midseventies, record sales have
steadily declined. Fewer and fewer people invest in turntables, pre-
ferring instead the convenience and portability of cassette players.
The wave of piracy that helped to wipe out the music industry in
Sierra Leone threatens to do the same in Ghana. Many entrepreneurs have set up sophisticated cassette duplicating studios to feed
the public's entertainment appetite. From such businesses the artists who made the music receive nothing. "It hurts a great deal,"
Ampadu complains. "This has been a battle between the musicians
or the copyright owners and those piraters. We are still trying to
find a way of . . . accepting them and taking some token fees from
them to continue with their job. Because they are eating into the
system, into the rural areas, everywhere. [But] we feel if we intend
to stop them it must cause a havoc. Because most of us haven't got

the right inputs to feed the people with the cassette on our own accord. So we are thinking of charging them a fee periodically so they can continue with the job."

In spite of mounting difficulties, Ampadu keeps his home base in Ghana. While many of his contemporaries have fled to supposedly greener pastures in Europe and America, often with disastrous results, he rejects this path. He works instead to maintain his status as one of Ghana's leading entertainers, figuring that a strong reputation earned at home buttressed by recordings and occasional international tours will eventually bring wider acclaim. "I feel that it is better to be great in one's own country," he says, "than to be great in somebody's country and be rejected in your own."

High Times, Hard Times

Hedzoleh Soundz

9

The future looked bright for the Ghanaian band Hedzoleh Soundz in 1973. It was the reigning band at the popular Napoleon Club in Accra, an album recorded with Hugh Masekela would soon be released, and a promotional tour of the United States was in the offing. But the promise gradually evaporated in the heat of clashing egos and misunderstanding—a testament to the power and perversity of an illusion held by many African musicians, that of easy success and wealth in the West.

The demise of Hedzoleh Soundz was doubly tragic, because for them the opportunity was real. Masekela and his producer and business partner Stewart Levine, old friends and collaborators since their student days at the Manhattan School of Music in the early sixties, were touring West Africa in 1973 searching for musicians. "Our problem right through the sixties," Levine recalls, "was that we could never get the proper musicianship. The American musicians, . . . guys who had enough chops, like the jazz musicians, to play the music we wanted to, were sort of jaded and didn't really know how to play with the groove, and the African music really put them off. And the guys who could play with a groove, like the sort of R & B guys, were not sophisticated enough to play the African music. So we were very frustrated. Although we were making African-American records right through from '65 on, we never felt that we really captured what we were looking after because of the lack of musicians."[1]

But in Hedzoleh Soundz they found it. "Those guys completely knocked us out," Levine continues. "They just had everything that when you closed your eyes you would expect to come out of Africa. You know? It was just rhythmically incredible. The instrumentation was odd in a great way. They didn't even have real traps. You

79

know, the drummer . . . just had a bass drum and some sort of tuned bells and cymbals. There wasn't a snare drum, and there wasn't, you know, traditional Western instruments weren't there. It just was exciting. Two conga drummers, bass player, and guitar player. No keyboards, you know, it was wide open."

Hedzoleh Soundz had begun to form in Accra in 1971 with bassist Amartey "Lash" Laryea and musician-sculptor Saka Acquaye, who were brought together by their mutual desire to develop a new musical style relying more on original compositions played with traditional African instruments and less on Western pop sounds. The mimicking of rock and soul was the rage for over a decade beginning around the midsixties. Groups like the Heartbeats from Sierra Leone who toured the West African coast and local bands—the Barbecues, El Pollos, Circuit Five, and others—all built tremendous followings to the tune of Western hits. Laryea and Acquaye wanted to go in a different direction. They enlisted conga players James Kwaku Morton and Nat "Lee Puma" Hammond, drummer Acheampong "Salas" Welbeck, percussionist Sammy Nortey, and guitarist Niisai "Jagger" Botchway and began to rehearse together.

Trouble developed early as Acquaye, who acted as the group's manager and musical director, and Laryea began to clash. "Lash was another character, right?" says drummer Okyerema Isaac Asante, who joined the group soon after it formed. "He couldn't get along with a lot of people. And that caused misunderstanding between him and Saka Acquaye. So Saka Acquaye pulled out."[2]

To fill the void left by Acquaye's departure, the group contacted businessman Faisal Helwani, a Ghanaian of Lebanese descent, who owned F Promotions and the Napoleon Club discotheque. Helwani had been looking for a band to play at the Napoleon in order to infuse some new life into the disco scene, so the group "did a little demo for him." Drummer Salas Welbeck remembers, "He listened to it, listened to it, listened to it, said this is something he can sell. That's a good product he can sell. . . . So he looked at it, listened to it, said, 'Well all right, come on. You don't have money, I'll buy you equipment.' And that's where we started."[3]

The musicians put their full energy into the new venture, rehearsing seven hours a day, experimenting, composing, tightening up the act. Helwani managed and promoted the group and instilled

Hedzoleh Soundz in happier times: (*left to right*) Acheampong "Salas" Welbeck, James Kwaku Morton, Faisal Helwani, Sammy Nortey, Paajoe Amissah, and Nat "Lee Puma" Hammond. Photo courtesy of Hedzoleh Soundz

a sense of discipline. "If you don't show up to rehearsal, you don't get paid," says Welbeck. Helwani took a chance, recalls Paajoe Amissah, who worked in Accra with bands like Sweet Beans and the Millionaires and now plays bass with the remnants of Hedzoleh in California. "When everybody was busy playing rock and roll, they were talking about xylophones and calabash drums, so it was a big risk. . . . But Faisal believed in the whole concept."[4] Nevertheless, Helwani's talents as promoter and businessman failed him in the area of personal relationships. Communication was poor, particularly where money was concerned. "If somebody asked a question about the money and things like that, he would get offended," says Asante. Lash Laryea eventually quit in just such a dispute, and bassist Stanley Todd was brought in to replace him.

Despite personality conflicts, the band's rise was rapid. From its debut in 1971 it kept up a grueling pace rehearsing, playing live gigs, and recording. The group's adaptation of an old West African folk song became the hit record "Rekpete," and they recorded music for the Italian film *Contact*. Their nightly shows packed the Napoleon Club.

The musicians remember the Napoleon with great fondness. It resembled a castle and contained a bar and restaurant and a large indoor garden complete with plants and caged birds where patrons could relax with food and drink. The dance floor was lit with black lights so the dancers' clothing would appear to glow in the darkness. Early evening hours were for eating and drinking and dancing to the latest records from around the world. Hedzoleh Soundz would come on around eleven P.M. and play until two A.M., and then records would again take over until dawn. The popular Napoleon helped to enliven the capital's flourishing nightlife in the early seventies.

In 1973 Masekela and Levine visited Liberia and then traveled on to Lagos as guests of afro-beat pioneer Fela Anikulapo-Kuti. Nigerian music sounded too Westernized for their purposes, so Fela took them to Accra, where they wound up at the Napoleon Club listening to Hedzoleh Soundz. "We were playing there at the club one day," Asante recalls, "and we saw Fela walking in with this short man and this tall white man in dashiki with an afro hair. . . . We didn't know who they were." After the show the players went upstairs to Helwani's office and were introduced to the visitors. Masekela loved the highly percussive sound Hedzoleh had developed, and he was invited to sit in with the group. "The next day when he was coming, he brought his flugelhorn," says Asante. "And he came and sat in for a set with that . . . I mean he just jumped in with that and wow! We say, 'Whoa!' The music was just changed. We said, 'Goddam! Look at this! This man change all our music.' So we also love him."

A deal was quickly struck for a joint recording of Masekela and Hedzoleh to be followed by a promotional tour of the United States. In July 1973 the group went into the EMI studios in Lagos and recorded the album *Masekela: Introducing Hedzoleh Soundz.* "In fact," says Levine, "when we made that record we basically took their thing, and Hughie basically played their music, which was what the intention was. . . . Hugh just basically sat in with them, I would say."

The recording studio was a quirky eight-track facility complete with an engineer who kept falling asleep. "The studio was interesting," Levine says, sounding somewhat amused at his recollection. "They had these really expensive condenser microphones. . . . And

Okyerema Asante. Photo courtesy of Okyerema Asante

they were completely useless. That's why all the records over there
sounded like shit, because these microphones would pick up everything. So I talked Fela into giving me, borrowing, a whole bunch of
stage mikes, like dynamic mikes, very cheap mikes which are used
in PA systems. We rewired them, and we used them in the studio to
get really tight sort of miking like I used to do with my R & B records. . . . I was shocked when we got it back to L.A. [where Masekela overdubbed his parts] and it sounded as good as it did."

Masekela's recollections of this period are harder to come by. He
doesn't like to be interviewed. "A lot of writers write a lot of
things," he said when refusing a request to talk, the inference being
that they aren't always accurate. He says he has signed a deal with
Simon & Schuster to write his autobiography: "All what I have to
say I'm gonna put in there." He does, however, talk during his
shows. He is fond of playing Fela's song "Lady." He dedicates it to
Fela and recalls for audiences the months of 1973 he spent in West
Africa: "Those were some of the best times of my life."

For his part, Fela was only too happy to help as long as he could be sure that whatever band was selected would be treated fairly. "You see, okay, if they came and wanted to record and take the tape away, I wouldn't have helped them," he says. "But they wanted to take a band, and that's the kind of thing I like for my people. If you want to take my people on a journey, that's good. But I hate people, I hate artists coming and just using the [African] artists to record and bring the tapes [abroad]."[5]

In late December, the album had been released and the tour booked, and the band took off for the States full of anticipation. They opened January 4, 1974 in Washington, D.C., and proceeded to play for large audiences all across the country. "I brought them to thank Africa for giving me inspiration," Masekela told Arlynn Nellhaus of the *Denver Post*. "I wanted to bring them out because of the respect I have for them—no matter how much they will be exploited. . . . This will be the next vogue."[6]

Behind the scenes, however, problems flared up almost immediately. "When we got here [to the United States], that's where the real problems started," says Asante. "We got here with the idea in mind that here is where the action is. Here, musician, if you're here you make a million in two weeks. Everything here means a musician, you make a lot of money. There's no hardship for musician." As Asante tells it, many in the group drank heavily and abused their telephone and food expense accounts. "You know, these guys, they would get up in the morning, they would go downstairs at breakfast time, somebody would order maybe six shots of whiskey," he says. Levine remembers that some in the band were doing drugs: "They didn't take too well to coming out here really. A couple of them were all right, and a couple of them weren't. [The band] had their own internal problems."

One problem was that Helwani demanded 25 percent of each musician's hundred-dollar weekly allowance. Another was that much of the publicity featured Masekela's name prominently— often to the exclusion of the name Hedzoleh—which upset Helwani since he hoped the tour would break his band into the American market. Disharmony intensified with each passing city. "The whole thing comes back to understanding," says Asante. "It was just simple understanding, you know, communication, talk with people. . . . Faisal got fed up, so it was always like a fight. . . . So it got to the point the group also got attitude. So the road was like, instead of being happy on the road, it was like, ha! you want to tear each other's throat." Whatever the truth is about all the backstage conflicts, when the group reached San Francisco a bitter Helwani left the tour and returned to Ghana.

There were other concerns as well. Levine recalls that "it cost a fortune to keep [the tour] going," and record sales were disappointing. "The record didn't happen," he says. "It was an ambitious work. We're talking about 1974, you know. We didn't know that African music wouldn't even be looked at for another fifteen years at least, you know. We had our heads in the sand, and we were very, very much into what we were doing and thought we had a shot with this record."

The next stop, Los Angeles, was a busy one for the group. They opened at the Troubadour Club to a star-studded audience that included Marvin Gaye, Stevie Wonder, and Little Richard. In between club dates they appeared on the popular television program "Soul Train" and recorded tracks for a new Masekela album called *I Am Not Afraid.*

In the midst of all this activity, concerns over money became stronger. Some members of the group felt they had not been paid all they were due. Never party to the business arrangements among Masekela, Levine, and Helwani, the players were unsure about who was really looking after them. Although there was a last stop in Seattle and plans for another album after the group had returned to Accra to write new material, the members of Hedzoleh Soundz decided to stay in Los Angeles. "We don't want to go," says Welbeck. "You know, hey! What's wrong with your own home? You gonna run from you home? No! But the idea is, where is the money, 'cause we have children back home. You just snatch me from my family and then coming home empty-handed, that's crazy. . . . So we say okay, we're gonna hang in here and try to make it on our own."

The rest of 1974 and much of 1975 was spent just trying to survive. Since the band had mostly been using rented instruments on the tour, they had few of their own with which to play. Help that had been promised by prominent Ghanaians living in Los Angeles failed to materialize. The players wound up working in an aircraft parts factory to support themselves. Three members, Stanley Todd, Jagger Botchway, and Asante, rejoined Masekela to record more albums including *The Boy's Doin' It* and *Colonial Man* with Masekela's new "find," Orlando Julius Ekemode of Nigeria.

The four remaining members recruited Paajoe Amissah to play bass and migrated north to the San Francisco area. They played nightclubs and jammed with Joni Haastrup and Ekemode, who himself had split with Masekela. Success however, was tempered by bad luck, bad management, and sometimes outright deceit. The group spurned separate offers of work from both Helwani and Masekela. A successful concert tour ended in dispute with the musicians accusing their new American manager of stealing the proceeds. The master tape for a new album was lost for a time when the recording studio went bankrupt. Although the tape was later recovered, the players have failed to raise enough money to finish it.

Dispute and disappointment have taken their toll. The remaining members of the group are scattered about northern California, working odd jobs, getting together for an occasional gig, hoping for the magic and promise of 1973 to return. The world of commercial music is capricious at best, however, and while African music is increasingly popular, the big money goes to a new generation of musicians and a few old established stars. It remains to be demonstrated that an African band based in the United States can achieve a measure of fame and fortune on the level of Kanda Bongo Man, Fela, or Sonny Okosuns.

The Beat Goes On

Olatunji

10

Happening as it did in Marin County, the event was surprising. The sound of African drums pierced the quiet dusk of the affluent, mostly white northern California enclave. A gaggle of suburbanites, their perspiring bodies arrayed with—or revealed by—trendy workout gear, strutted with a mixture of awkwardness and grace to the syncopated exhortations of an ensemble of African dancers and drummers. Presiding over the unlikely spectacle, with the aplomb of an indulgent professor, was Nigeria's master drummer Babatunde Olatunji.

The road version of Olatunji's Center of African Culture was touring again, performing and teaching with missionary zeal. Created in the midsixties with earnings from his dazzling performances at the New York World's Fair, the center was a fixture on Harlem's 125th Street. But hard times—high rents and lack of city government support—have forced it to become a floating conservatory of culture, holding classes in various short-term locations and conducting business from a cramped Broadway office suite.

Even worse than his cultural center's homelessness has been his recording career's eclipse. Although live performance is the essence of African music, recording is the lifeblood of American success. For twenty years Olatunji's drums of passion produced no new records—that is, until he met Mickey Hart of the Grateful Dead. Their collaboration has reopened record executives' eyes and recording studio doors. Hart still remembers his first encounter with Olatunji's music during high school in the late fifties: "He was the first one that I heard use talking drums or variable pitched drums in his performance, you know, in African performance. And he mixed the African performance with the urban New York music. And it was the combination, brass and percussion and voice, that changed the way I thought about drums."[1]

Olatunji's influence covers a span of nearly four decades. As Africa's self-appointed ambassador of culture, he has attempted to correct Americans' Tarzan-inspired misconceptions and fought to protect African traditions from Western cultural dominance. To see his troupe of drummers and dancers is to experience the uninhibited exuberance and excitement of Africa. The ensemble often begins a performance by entering through the audience. Olatunji leads the graceful processional, smiling and shaking hands with friends and fans. The performers are engulfed in a sea of bodies writhing as if one to the powerful beat of the drums.

Emerging from the crowd, Olatunji takes center stage behind two huge, chest-high drums surrounded by the rest of the dozen or so cast members. Guitars, bass, and keyboards eschew melody to play their own percussion chops in support of the African drums. Suddenly the audience parts as a giant stilt dancer rises up as if by magic. Male and female dancers in a dazzling, ever-changing profusion of costumes undulate across the stage, gracefully bending and contorting their bodies in impossible shapes, to enact the story of an initiation or marriage. Throughout it all, Olatunji pounds his drums and chants ancient invocations to the gods, propelling his troupe to a higher level of energy.

Music is vital to the culture of Olatunji's Yoruba people of western Nigeria; he has been playing, singing, and dancing almost from the day he was born. "The music covers all the vicissitudes of life," he says. "When a child is born there's music and dance. When you reach the age of puberty, that is also celebrated."[2]

It seems ironic, but he is, in part, a product of one of the catalysts of African cultural disintegration, the Christian missionary church. But unlike Okonkwo in Chinua Achebe's *Things Fall Apart*,[3] Olatunji managed to reconcile Christianity and traditional culture. As a youth in the thirties and forties, he attended an American mission school in Nigeria's capital, Lagos, where he was christened Michael.

American missionaries, although clearly intent on saving "heathen" Africans from themselves, were at least less rigid than their English counterparts. Among other things, Olatunji recalls, the Church of England forbade the use of drums in religious services.

The African Methodist Episcopal Church evolved under the tutelage of American missionaries to accommodate both Christianity and African tradition. "In the psalms," he points out, "they say, 'Praise the Lord with all the instruments.' This [the drum] is our main instrument." As he speaks in a dingy Oakland, California, nightclub dressing room he begins to sing "Onward, Christian Soldiers" in the Yoruba language while beating an intricate rhythm on the countertop—the roots of gospel laid bare.

Olatunji parlayed his mission school education into a promising civil service career in the British colonial administration of Nigeria. But despite his job in the Labor Department, he found time to play music with local groups and the theatrical troupe of Hubert Ogunde, father of Nigerian musical theater. Following World War II, much to the displeasure of colonial authorities, Ogunde's productions carried the message of nationalism throughout Nigeria. Olatunji joined the troupe whenever they performed near his post

DMS Communication Design / San Francisco

in eastern Nigeria. "There was a national purpose at that time of getting independence," he remembers. "A unity of purpose of making Nigeria one." Independence would not come for more than a decade, however, and Olatunji would be fighting other battles in America.

He came to the United States in 1950 on a scholarship from the Rotary Educational Foundation of Atlanta, Georgia. Of his transatlantic voyage from Lagos to New Orleans he says, "I came here like most black Americans came, except that I was not chained." Totally unprepared for the Jim Crow South, he was bewildered to find himself forcibly separated from his white shipmates, with whom he had mingled freely at sea. Rides in an all-black train car and a blacks-only taxi delivered him to Atlanta's all-black and all-male Morehouse College.

Racial segregation was bewildering to Olatunji, but Americans' ignorance of Africa was alarming. "The questions they were asking me in our freshman year were questions enough to force you to want to go back home," he recalls. "But I knew somehow, by intuition I said, 'They're really serious. They really mean business. They want to know. They are genuine questions. They are not trying to be sarcastic. They are ignorant.'"

Olatunji plunged into his studies, sandwiching courses in education and social studies between chorus, glee club, football (for a few days at least), and, eventually, a stint as student body president. He earned spending money speaking and playing in local churches, including some white ones, in a kind of missionary role reversal. In 1953 he put together a troupe of Africans and black Americans to give his first full-scale cultural performance.

Following graduation in 1954, Olatunji moved north to begin a Ph.D. program in public administration at New York University. He met and married his American wife, and they began to raise a family that would eventually include four children. At the conclusion of three years of course work he selected a dissertation topic: "Critical Analysis of the Impact of Colonial Administration on the Communal Ownership of Land and How It Has Affected Capital Development and Capital Formation in Nigeria from 1900 to 1950." But there was no money to do research in Nigeria.

Suddenly music had a fresh attraction. Throughout college, his music and cultural performances were constantly in demand, so he

Babatunde Olatunji. Photo courtesy of Babatunde Olatunji

shelved the dissertation proposal to concentrate exclusively on an entertainment career. Word of his sensational shows reached a representative of Columbia Records who, sensing the makings of a new trend (the fifties, thanks to Harry Belafonte, was already experiencing a calypso craze), signed him to a recording contract in 1958—an act that reportedly cost the adventurous Columbia employee his job.

The Columbia brass needn't have worried. *Drums of Passion,* Olatunji's first album, sold well (Olatunji says over five million; a spokesperson for CBS puts the figure closer to two hundred thousand) and is still in print. But he maintains the contract's penurious terms effectively denied him royalties. Earnings were greater from Santana's performance of one of the album's songs, "Jin-Go-Lo-Ba," than they were from Olatunji's own rendering. He laughs at the irony. Nevertheless, *Drums of Passion* was great exposure that enhanced his stature as a performer.

"On October 22, 1960," wrote Africanist Robert Farris Thompson, "a remarkable scene unfolded at the Village Gate nightclub in New York. While a Nigerian musician flailed his drums, with sly and piercing percussive wit, Jack Kerouac (in an alcove unseen by a vast audience of intellectuals, college students, and just plain expense accounters) answered the drumming with a private mambo, assisted by two females."[4] Olatunji and his ensemble had become part of the city's in-crowd.

Buoyed by the success of *Drums of Passion,* Columbia agreed to release a second LP, *Zungo,* in 1961. With *Zungo* Olatunji recreated what had taken place in Africa decades earlier, the synthesis of Western instruments and jazz riffs with African percussion and call and response singing. Yusef Lateef, Clark Terry, and George Duvivier were among a host of distinguished contributors to the album.

Legendary producer John Hammond presided over further recording sessions that yielded two LPs, *Flaming Drums* and *High Life.* More jazz greats including Hosea Taylor, Snookie Young, Bob Brookmeyer, and Ray Barretto wove their wizardry through Olatunji's enchanting rhythms. *High Life,* a wonderful rendition of the West African highlife style popularized in the forties and fifties by Ghanaians like E. T. Mensah, suffered from its uninspired cover, which featured a bland photo of Olatunji with a white female model. Appearing as it did in the midst of America's racial turmoil, it was, according to Olatunji, the kiss of death.

Wind player Lateef signed on as the group's music director, and they played regularly in some of New York's most famous nightspots including Cafe Au Go Go and Birdland. Saxophone great John Coltrane, whose obsession with drums and rhythm was evident in his percussion-driven performances, took a particular liking to Olatunji. In the African music and language Coltrane seemed to find new inspiration and a cultural grounding he had not known before. He wrote a song called "Tunji" for his friend and was a co-founder and steadfast supporter of Olatunji's Center of African Culture.

But African music, a refreshing novelty in 1960s America, clearly would never be mainstream. African derivatives like jazz and rock and roll were where the money was to be made. Columbia began to lose interest. Olatunji managed to wheedle the recording of two more albums, *Drums! Drums! Drums!* in 1964 for Roulette and *More Drums of Passion* in 1966 for Columbia, before the record moguls' attention spans snapped.

For the next two decades he concentrated on nurturing his cultural center and doing research. He wrote two books, *Musical Instruments of Africa* with Betty Warner Dietz and *Yoruba Ode Oni,* and assisted with CBS documentaries on Haitian and Nigerian culture. Each year he spent enormous amounts of time on the road—often back home in Africa—lecturing at colleges and universities, doing workshops and nightclub shows, "preparing the way," he explains, "for those who are now coming to perform, Sunny Ade, all the rest of them."

All the while, says Olatunji, frustration welling in his voice, "I'd gone to all the [record] labels say, 'Look, my head is full of music, you know, give me a one deal contract.' I went back to my old CBS [Columbia]; they said no. The guy told me say he's not interested in my kind of music. I said, 'Look, I can do contemporary as well as traditional.' I went everywhere. People that I've known, they won't give me." Then he met the Grateful Dead.

Olatunji played a club date in San Francisco in 1985. In the audience was the Dead's drummer Mickey Hart. Olatunji recalls with great relish, "He came to find me and said, 'I remember you. . . . You haven't done anything lately. I know about your *Drums of Passion.* What are you doing?' I said, 'We are performing.' He said I'm going to hear from him. So two months later he called, 'Please come and open for the Grateful Dead New Year's Eve 1985.' That's how the whole cycle began again."

The collaboration didn't end there. "After January first [1986]," Olatunji continues, "he called me to his house and said, 'Look, I don't want you to go back to the East Coast. Before you go I have

ten days for you in the studio. Do anything you want to do.'" Hart
downplays his own role, saying simply, "He had to be recorded, so
we just did it." He adds, "Whenever I get a chance to play with
Olatunji, I do. Because after you finish playing with him you feel
really clean. You know? You feel like you've really played."

Suddenly it was like old times again with stars of other musical
styles like Hart, Carlos Santana, and Airto Moreira flocking to record with Olatunji. The ten-day session, digitally recorded at Fan-
tasy's state-of-the-art studio in Berkeley, California, produced
enough material for two albums; the twenty-year drought was
broken.

First to hit the record stores was *Dance to the Beat of My Drum*,
released in the fall of 1986 on the fledgling Blue Heron label and
later rereleased on Rykodisc as *Drums of Passion: The Beat*. Heavy
on percussion but featuring guitars more prominently than before,
Beat is mesmerizing, often sounding like juju music. Each of its five
songs is an extended jam running anywhere from nearly seven minutes to beyond twelve. The album's centerpiece is a remake of
"Akiwowo," chant to the trainman, from the original *Drums of Passion* album. It features a lush a cappella introduction and a Santana
solo that transforms his guitar into something like an electric talking drum that exhorts the trainman to bring the people home
safely.

Santa's Midi guitar synthesizer provides sweet, flute-like accom-
paniment to "Loyin Loyin," an upbeat, high-energy prayer for
Nigeria. A guitar quartet of Alfred C. Redwine, Frank Ekeh,
Joseph Bruce Langhorne, and Santana taking the lead propels "Se
Eni a Fe L'Amo—Kere Kere," a nine-minute juju groove based on
the African penchant for communication through proverb.

The second LP, *Drums of Passion: The Invocation*, has also been
released on Rykodisc and together with *The Beat* forms part of a
Mickey Hart–produced series entitled *The World*. *Invocation* contains six prayers chanted to Yoruba *orisas*—human beings who in
life so distinguished themselves that in death they have become a
means to communicate with God. One song segues into the next as
Olatunji's voice booms out over the layered rhythms, his incanta-
tions echoed by a chorus in characteristic call and response fashion.
Only Bobby Vega's bass accompanies the singing and drumming.

Prayers like those to Sango, god of thunder and lightning, and Kori, goddess of fertility, cast a trance-inducing spell, starting slowly, gradually increasing the tempo, building the rhythms and chants to a frenzied climax. Just as he did with *Drums of Passion* and *More Drums of Passion*—possibly his best album—Olatunji plants *Invocation* firmly on traditional ground, drawing sustenance from his cultural heritage, imparting its wisdom to the world.

Olatunji fervently believes that preservation of its culture will be Africa's salvation. Paradoxically (it would seem, in light of his Christianity and longtime U.S. residence), he is critical of African scholars and politicians who overlook what they have at home, studying instead Western models of culture and development. His life's work—the research, the lectures, and most of all the music—is, of course, his riposte to any suggestion of contradiction. Traditions are breaking down, he says: "We can safeguard against that breakdown if we continue to emphasize and to preserve, which is what I'm trying to do with the music."

Not surprisingly, he feels a strong need to convey the importance of their ancestry to African-Americans and is frustrated but understanding of the fact that his message is more readily accepted by whites. Black people are still struggling for survival, he says: "It's going to take time for African-Americans to be able to afford it, to be able to realize how important it is for them to know of their heritage."

Other frustrations are born of intrigues peculiar to the entertainment industry. He recorded some percussion tracks for the producers of Eddie Murphy's film *Coming to America,* an experience that left him increasingly bitter about show business ethics. "They [the film's producers] said give [them] some different rhythms. They'll listen, then they'll call," Olatunji says. The next thing he knew, his rhythms turned up mixed with other music in a completed film without his counsel or consent.

Another Olatunji project, Voices of Africa, has been stymied by lack of money. He envisions Voices as an annual series of fund-raising concerts, by Africans for Africans, to promote small-scale village projects like wells, farm assistance, scholarships, and medical clinics. "People have been helping Africans; when are Africans really going to help themselves?" he asks. But despite an illustrious board of directors and commitments to perform from several top African stars, the money needed to stage an inaugural concert has been tough to come by.

But the gloom of frustration and discouragement is always tempered by the exhilaration of a new challenge. Whether it be drumming with Mickey Hart, recording music for movie soundtracks, or dazzling audiences with his nightclub spectacle, Babatunde Olatunji shows no sign of slowing down. He was given his charge, he says with pride, in 1958. The previous year he had been elected president of the All-African Students' Union of the Americas, an event that somehow came to the attention of President Kwame Nkrumah of Ghana. As part of his Pan-Africanist vision, Nkrumah was organizing the first All-African People's Conference, and he invited Olatunji to be a delegate. Gathered in Accra in December 1958 were the world's black elite: George Padmore, Cheikh Anta Diop, W. E. B. DuBois, Patrice Lumumba, Julius Nyerere, Tom Mboya. "They were all nationalists at that time," says Olatunji, lowering his voice to emphasize the earnestness of his message. "So if I had pursued political aspirations I could have been in any position of those people. It was Nkrumah who told me, 'Please hold on to the culture, we're going to need it.'"

The Dawn of Afro-Beat

Orlando Julius Ekemode

11

The year was 1958—a decade after E. T. Mensah brought highlife to Nigeria—when sixteen-year-old Orlando Julius Ekemode blew his first notes on the saxophone. Nigeria's music scene was bubbling. Pop bands multiplied; *gramophone* became a household word. And there was talk of political independence.

O. J. was born to a Nigeria shackled by British colonialism. Coerced by foreign occupation and cajoled by missionaries of Christianity and Islam, Nigerians adapted in self-defense. Music, the vernacular of daily life, reflected the cultural accommodation. New forms for religious songs developed as Christian hymns collided with Nigeria's tonal languages and Islam's lack of melody ran up against indigenous musical tradition. School marching bands mimicked those of military brigades. Dance bands entertained colonial elites with highlifes, waltzes, and fox-trots. Percussion bands sprang up playing konkoma, apala, and sakara—styles derived from traditional music. Juju was born of the encounter between Yoruba music and West African palm wine guitar. Radio and records bombarded the country with new sounds.

Jazz Romero was a highlife musician living in the western Nigerian town of Ibadan. Romero was actually Ademola Haastrup who, like his contemporaries, exhibited a flair for coining stage names to rival that of Hollywood's most imaginative press agents. O. J.'s encounter with him was brief but memorable. O. J. had left his home in near-by Ijebu-Ijesa after dropping out of school, and despite his parents' objections had come to town to be a musician. He began to hang around Romero in hopes of getting some free lessons. "By that time I used to come to his house to do laundry, cook, and do all kinds of cleaning," he recalls. "So from there he got more interested in teaching me."[1]

O. J.'s eagerness and his work with local juju and konkoma bands won him a job playing trap drums with Romero's band at the Modupe Hotel in Ondo, a hundred or so miles southeast of Ibadan. Romero taught him two keys on the saxophone and O. J. graduated to playing second horn. Unfortunately, Romero was almost always in difficulty of one sort or another. He was forced to sell his trumpet to settle a fine soon after arriving in Ondo. The band then moved on to Akure, where Romero provoked a fight with the nightclub owner who had hired him. In a fit of anger or embarrassment he walked out on the band in the middle of the night. At the club owner's urging, O. J. took over as leader. "The guy who only knows two keys want to lead a band, gosh," he chuckles. "This boy who plays guitar and sings, Shadow Abraham, he knows [only] one chord."

The band soon fell apart. O. J. returned to Ibadan and managed to catch on with Rex Williams's band. Williams was a trumpet player from Calabar, in eastern Nigeria, who composed highlife songs in the language of that region's Efik people. O. J. found refuge in the horn section, where he could practice his craft without the burden of leadership. "There was no school of music," he says, "so I decided to buy records. Listen to Ghana records and listen to John Coltrane and listen to all kinds of records that have horns. Just put it on, and play it by ear." Ghanaian records were especially instructive for highlife, which, thanks to the Tempos, had become popular in Nigeria ten years earlier.

The 1948 visit of E. T. Mensah's Tempos had been a turning point for Nigerian music. The Tempos' mixture of sweet-sounding horns and African rhythms was captivating. By the midfifties highlife had become the rage. Many a trumpet player developed as Nigerian musicians rushed to emulate the great Ghanaian. Colonial elites and their Nigerian counterparts danced the highlife from Lagos to Calabar in clubs like Ambassador's, Wayfarer's and the West End Hotel. A correspondent for *West African Review* summed it up in 1959: "If you want an exhilarating, if somewhat exhausting, evening of uninhibited dancing, where no one looks askance if you muddle up the waltz with the tango, where women aren't looking each other up and down with catty eyes, and where anyone can excuse-me anyone else's partner, then a Night Out in Lagos is for you."[2]

Orlando Julius Ekemode (playing saxophone) and his Modern Aces circa 1966.
Photo courtesy of Orlando Julius Ekemode

Highlife invigorated the Western-style dance bands; it also tran-
scended ethnic differences. The juju music of I. K. Dairo and his
Blue Spots, Ayinde Bakare and his Rhythm Dandies, and others
was based in Yoruba culture. Highlife, on the other hand, incorporated rhythms and languages from the entire country. Efiks like Rex
Williams, Igbos like Rex Lawson, Yorubas Bobby Benson and
Victor Olaiya—all played highlife and staffed their bands based
not on ethnic origin but on musical talent and skill.

As O. J.'s playing improved, the word spread until it reached
bandleader Eddie Okonta. Okonta and his Top Aces were one of
Nigeria's best highlife bands, rivals of Victor Olaiya and his Cool
Cats and Roy Chicago and his Abalabi Rhythm Dandies. In 1960,
the year Nigeria gained its independence from Britain, Okonta of-
fered O. J. a job—an offer that was irresistible. "By that time Eddie
Okonta is a top band, a top-rated band in West Africa," says O. J.
"We even played so many gigs with [American jazzman] Cozy
Cole. We opened for Louis Armstrong when he came to Nigeria."

In the old days a good band could labor for years in the relative
obscurity of its own geographical area. But the spread of cheap ra-

dios and record players in the late fifties and early sixties changed
the situation considerably. Critic Albert McKay observed in 1957
that "West Africa seems to be sharing in the great post-war boom in
gramophone records, and the high-life has arrived as a valuable
commercial commodity."[3] To get close to the source, foreign record companies like EMI (owners of the His Master's Voice label),
Senafone, and Decca set up shop in Nigeria. Local businessmen
also got into the act, recording and releasing records independently
and sometimes acting in concert with the foreign companies.[4] A hit
record could suddenly catapult an unknown band to national
prominence. Recording and radio air play became essential means
for artists to sustain their popularity.

O. J. recorded several songs with Okonta's Top Aces and free-
lanced with other musicians. Recording sessions resembled live
performances since the musicians were recorded all at once. Studio
mixing boards could accommodate only a few microphones, so
singers and instrumentalists were grouped to produce the best balance. The live sound was mixed to a monophonic tape recorder. No
overdubs were possible on this single-track setup; a blunder by one
meant the entire band had to be rerecorded. Mistakes sometimes
led to creation of a new arrangement that surpassed the original.

Playing and recording with a top highlife band was wonderful
experience, but O.J. was a traditionalist. "From late '58 to '60 I'd
gone through many changes," he says, "you know, many bands.
And I didn't really like playing too much highlife music by that
time. I like to learn, [but] all my goal was just . . . to put traditional
that I started with, and add a little bit of horns and guitar, and then
do my own thing." His own thing turned out to be the Modern
Aces.

With help from juju guitarist I. K. Dairo, O. J. acquired some
instruments and began to recruit musicians for his own band. O. J.
remembers it was 1962; liner notes from one of his album say
1964. Whatever the year, Orlando Julius and his Modern Aces
made their debut at the Independence Hotel in Ibadan. The band
walked a fine line playing highlife and popular Western styles while
gently nudging the music closer to African roots.

Was it afro-beat in the making? This is a question that has provoked some heat between O. J. and fellow Nigerian Fela

Anikulapo-Kuti. O. J. remembers Fela as a frequent visitor to Modern Aces gigs in Ibadan. "He always stand near the stage with his trumpet [this was before Fela switched to saxophone] . . . and just play along. So by that time I really like the way he played trumpet. I always go and pull him on the stage to play." But, says O. J., in those

Orlando Julius Ekemode. Photo courtesy of Orlando Julius Ekemode

days "he was playing jazz. And later on he found out that he has to come back to his roots before he can be known. And already we were there."

For his part, Fela claims the name *afro-beat* (although O. J. says he used it first) and takes much of the credit for the music's popularity. As for counterclaims by others, Fela says, "It doesn't bother me, because I think I've left something for them to investigate and try to do the best they can. But I think I've gone past that, me. I've gone into more serious kind of thing now."[5]

A 1965 recording session for Philips West African Records produced O. J.'s first hit, a single called "Jagua Nana." *Jagua* was a slang term lifted from the British Jaguar sports car and satirically applied to Nana, a stereotypic woman. Nigerian novelist Cyprian Ekwensi explained it in a short story: "She was Jagua, which meant that she had style in everything she did. . . . It was girls like her who started fashions, and when these frivolities swept like angry flames to Lome, Bathurst, Freetown, and Lagos other girls would emulate."[6]

"Jagua Nana" gave the Modern Aces a tremendous boost. Invitations for the band to perform came from as far away as Ghana and Côte d' lvoire. The band began to tour and released another hit record called "Topless." When the soul sound of James Brown swept Nigeria, O. J. didn't miss a beat. He recorded the single "Ijo Soul" and later released an album called *Super Afro Soul* that featured an up-and-coming signer named Joni Haastrup who would go on to become Nigeria's "soul brother number one." For a bandleader, keeping abreast of swiftly changing trends was vital. As the Modern Aces grew and music styles came and went, O. J. formed companion groups, the Afro Sounders and later the Evelyn Dance Band, in an effort to keep pace with the public's changing musical tastes.

Civil war broke out in 1967, and Nigeria splintered along ethnic lines. The Igbo people, alleging maltreatment at the hands of Nigeria's central government, declared the Eastern Region to be the independent Republic of Biafra. Many of the country's bands dissolved or regrouped as their Igbo members left to join the secessionist movement. Some observers have declared that the war killed highlife and fostered the popularity of ethnic styles like juju. While the war was definitely a factor, the invasion of foreign music clearly shared responsibility for highlife's decline. The technological leap in production of Western music gave it a solid edge over the rough creations of Nigerian studios. Payola was also an element; some disc jockeys developed a "you pay we play" policy. Western music began to dominate the airwaves.

When the war ended in 1970, the country started to rebuild, but O. J. and the other musicians continued to be battered by foreign competition. International record companies that controlled the Nigerian music business profited most by importing records of their British and American stars. They did little to upgrade their Nigerian production facilities. O. J. remembers: "You can tell records that they produce over here and records that they produce over there, they sound different. So I didn't know the reason why. I know that there must be some better equipment, but I don't know, so I was really [curious]."

As O. J. saw it, substandard production facilities were hardly the only problem. The record companies' attempts to market the music internationally had failed. Records alone inadequately conveyed African music's visual and participatory spectacle. Film and television, he felt, were the missing ingredients. He decided to go abroad to learn more about record and film production.

O. J. made extensive travels through Europe in the early seventies with stops at Philips's studios and factories in Germany and Holland. Along the way he jammed with musical members of Europe's burgeoning Nigerian communities. But it was a 1973 visit to the United States with its abundance of recording and film production studios that captured his imagination. He wound up business in Nigeria and moved to America.

Bluesman Wild Child Butler once said, "I been got and I have paid so many dues. . . . I don't know when they'll stop. I'm still paying them. I don't know what's going to come out of it."[7] Paying one's dues is the musician's lot and the musician's lament. In America, O. J. paid his all over again. He settled in Washington, D.C., and formed a band called Umoja. Most of the musicians were African, but a few Americans caught on. American musicians were difficult, says O. J., because they were into funk and messed up the music.

For most of 1974 Umoja played the D.C. nightclub circuit, entertaining the cosmopolitan capital. Late in the year good fortune

appeared. Hugh Masekela, fresh from his falling out with
Hedzoleh Soundz, was in search of African musicians. He dropped
in on a rehearsal where Umoja was polishing O. J.'s ode to time,
"Ashiko." Impressed by what he heard, Masekela invited O. J. to
tour with him. A new band was formed with some members of
Umoja and a few holdovers from Hedzoleh.

Masekela's tour went on for most of 1975 and part of 1976. The
band opened for some of the biggest names in show business—
Herbie Hancock, the Pointer Sisters, Grover Washington—
playing venues like the Spectrum in Philadelphia and Carnegie
Hall. It was great exposure for African music. They recorded two
albums, *The Boy's Doin' It,* featuring O. J.'s "Ashiko," and *Colonial
Man.* But O. J. was dissatisfied. Having been a successful leader
himself, he chafed in his role as a mere sideman. He claims to have
received no royalties for his compositions; Masekela, he says, made
promises but failed to deliver. O. J. decided to strike out on his
own.

He did session work for a while in Los Angeles and landed a
small acting role in the television series "Roots: The Second Generation." In 1978 he moved north to Oakland, where he enrolled in
film school. A number of African musicians, including the
Nigerian "soul brother" Joni Haastrup, Hedzoleh Soundz, and
Cameroonian guitarist Jean Koh Elong, were in the area working
on their own projects. Along with O. J. they gathered occasionally
at a place called Michael's Den for jam sessions that are still fondly
remembered by many of those fortunate enough to have squeezed
into the tiny bar.

The enthusiastic crowds drawn to those performances renewed
O. J.'s hope that African music could eventually break into the
American market. He began to teach local musicians to play his
brand of afro-beat and formed a band called Ashiko. The task of
developing an African band without Africans was formidable. Africans, says O. J., take a distinctive approach toward music. "When I
play instrument it sounds different to the way Western people
would play it. Because our thinking, our singing, our arrangement,
everything comes from African music, which is a variety of different feelings, different styles. . . . If I'm playing the saxophone
solo, sometimes I'll be playing solo like when playing percussion,
African drumming, or African singing."

The band's personnel changed constantly; competition from funk and disco was fierce. Nevertheless, Ashiko developed a strong following. The struggle took its toll, however, and O. J. grew weary. He longed to work with African musicians who shared his culture and understood the music. In 1984 he decided to return home.

Back in Nigeria, O. J. was liberated from his teaching role. Working with the best Nigerian session personnel, he went into the belatedly modernized EMI studios to record the tracks for *Dance Afro-Beat*. The recording project led to formation of the Nigerian All Stars, and with the help of Shanachie Records, the album's distributor, a U.S. tour began to take shape. As part of the promotion, O. J.'s dream of presenting the full spectacle of African music came to fruition. He hired a video crew and traveled to Osogbo in the heart of Yorubaland. With the sacred shrine of the River Goddess Osun as a background, he shot the *Dance Afro-Beat* video.

Tour dates were booked, and in October of 1985 the eighteen-member Nigerian All Stars band landed in New York. But Shanachie had backed the tour intending to feature the All Stars along with their other Nigerian artists, the Lijadu Sisters. Incredibly, through misunderstanding which seems endemic to the music business, the Lijadus never arrived. After one performance the tour collapsed.

Since then the road has been uncertain. Several of the All Stars split off to work with other bands. A recording and promotional deal with a New York agency went sour, resulting in a quick death for an album called *Sisi Shade*. But O. J. and the remaining All Stars continue to persevere. The battle has been arduous, but when O. J. goes onstage he is transformed. "My music is very healing," he says. The pain subsides, and the soul is resurrected. Audiences soak up the salubrious energy. "That's what we're gonna be doing worldwide. Playing healing music and teaching people more about our culture."

Soul Brother Number One

Joni Haastrup

12

Soul music conquered Lagos in the 1960s, and Joni Haastrup was "soul brother number one." As the Clusters kicked into a James Brown groove, Haastrup would spring into action, gyrating in all directions, doing impossible dips, walking across the stage on one foot, while effortlessly belting out "Sex Machine" or "Say it Loud." Today the old moves are still there, but as leader of a new band called O'sha, playing the northern California nightclub circuit, soul brother Joni Haastrup is twenty years and ten thousand miles away from those heady days of rock and soul in Nigeria. His music is different too. The compositions are original now, the African roots more in evidence, but there is still a healthy helping of the rock sounds he loves so much.

Haastrup grew up in a royal household in the western Nigerian town of Ilesa. Originally named John, he decided early on to call himself Joni because it sounded more like Yoruba. And Yoruba he is despite the Dutch name Haastrup, a legacy of European transgressions in Africa.

Life in the royal household was a musical education. He remembers early morning visits to the compound by various drummers, *agidigbo* (bass thumb piano) players, even a bugler, who would come to honor his grandfather the *owa* (king) of Ijesaland. At night he often volunteered to be lamp carrier for bands of musicians who roamed the busy streets. "Even though I was growing up in a royal setting, I was always very curious to know what was happening on the outside," he recalls. "So I was actually blacklisted in the family as, you know, being the one who, I'm always out on the street trying to see what's going on. . . . When I actually started playing music, my mother told me I couldn't come back and claim her or claim to be her child."[1]

Haastrup learned to play traditional drums and picked up a few chords on the guitar, but singing and dancing were his real passions. He remembers happy times away from the royal compound at a record shop across the street from his father's house in Ilesa: "Every evening at about seven o'clock, they had big loudspeakers in front of the shop to, you know, to play this really loud music. And the people gather, and I'd be the only little kid in the center of the circle dancing."

As teenagers in the early sixties, Haastrup and his elder brother Segun formed a band called the Sneakers that played cover versions of pop hits from Europe and America. The Sneakers evolved into the Agriscol Harmoniers when they gained sponsorship from the School of Agriculture in nearby Akure and began to play for agriculture shows around the area. One such performance in 1965 proved to be a turning point in Haastrup's life.

Following an appearance by the group in Agege, a Lagos suburb, the two brothers stayed for a few days to check out the capital's music scene. They visited highlife bandleader Bobby Benson's Caban Bamboo Club, where Segun did a guitar audition in hopes of catching on with Benson's Jam Session Orchestra. Segun didn't make it, but Joni fared better the next afternoon during a pop jamboree at the Central Hotel. He sat in with the featured band and did a Chuck Berry number to cheers from the crowd and a rave review in one of the newspapers. Joni decided to stay in Lagos.

He attended Nigerian People's High School and performed with the school's drama society, which he founded as a ruse to get a band together. Through his performances with the school group, he came to the attention of "the evil genius of highlife," Victor Olaiya. Olaiya thought Haastrup's acrobatic dancing and frantic vocals were just what he needed to catch on with the soul craze that was sweeping Lagos. Haastrup joined up, and the highlife Cool Cats band became Victor Olaiya's All Stars Soul International. He sang and danced with the group for a year and a half, working on his James Brown repertoire and building a reputation as an electrifying performer.

By the late sixties, soul music flourished throughout western Nigeria. Despite blackouts and curfews, by-products of the country's civil war raging in the east, groups like the Strangers, Segun Bucknor and his Soul Assembly, and the Heartbeats from Sierra

Joni Haastrup. Photo courtesy of Joni Haastrup

Leone captured the youth. Another band trying to cash in on the soul phenomenon was Clusters International. It was a popular group but lacked a charismatic front man, so the members approached Haastrup about leaving Olaiya and bringing his soul brother act to them. Eager to front his own band, Haastrup agreed, and the Clusters were off and running toward the top. "We were hot!" he says. "The Clusters played everything and everybody. . . . We stayed as close to the original as possible. We made sure that when you heard it you thought you were hearing the record except that we had our own little innovations added to it."

Competition among the soul bands was keen. Promoter Chris Okolie would often book the Clusters and the Heartbeats on the same bill, a pairing that produced packed houses and sensational performances. "It was beautiful, it was wild, it was really wild," Haastrup recalls. "It was really good to have been involved in that for me, because all my confidence as far as being onstage grew out of all that competition, all the challenges that I experienced coming up as a singer."

While Western sounds were influencing music in Africa, African music was beginning to make its presence felt in the West. In England, for example, percussionists Remi Kabaka of Nigeria and

Ghana's Speedy Acquaye had worked with a number of musicians including rock drummer Ginger Baker. Baker had been fascinated by the polyrhythms of African music ever since he encountered the great Ghanaian drummer Guy Warren (now known as Kofi Ghanaba) in 1960 at a London jazz club called the Flamingo. Baker told journalist Valerie Wilmer, "When I went on to play he [Warren] produced this talking drum and asked if he could have a play. He came on and we had a ball. We played for about two hours and got the crowd screaming mad and that was the beginning of it all for me."[2]

In 1970 Baker traveled to Ghana and Nigeria for a firsthand look at the region and its music. In Lagos one evening, he saw Haastrup sitting in with the Hykkers at the Kakadu nightclub and was so impressed by the performance that he invited him to London to work.

Haastrup quickly accepted the offer and left the Clusters to join Baker's new group, Airforce. But there was a problem, he recalls with much amusement. "There was a lot of misconception about what I could do. When I went with Ginger, he saw me singing. He never saw me play an instrument, but he had this great belief within himself that I could play any instrument. So he wanted me to play the organ because Steve Winwood was leaving. And he also wanted me to play guitar because Denny Laine was leaving. So I got into London on a, I think on a Tuesday. The first gig was on Thursday. I have never heard the music of the band. I don't know what they sound like. I don't know anybody in the band but Ginger. I've never even heard Ginger play drums face-to-face except on record. He wants me to play organ and guitar and sing in this big ten-piece band with Graham Bond and Bud Beadle and all these people. And I uh, and I said, 'Well, Ginger I don't really play any of these instruments. I'm just a singer.' And he goes, 'Hey! You can do it. You can fuckin' do it'[laughter]."

The two went to Baker's house to listen to the group's music. Haastrup remembers having to listen from an entirely new perspective, that of an instrumentalist instead of a singer. "So I said, 'Okay, well, it will take me a couple of weeks to just listen and try to learn them.' He says, 'No, you've got two days.' And I say, 'Well fuck! Shit!' [laughs] I couldn't believe it. Two days!"

In the event, Haastrup played a little electric piano and guitar to start and wound up in the more familiar role of singer and dancer in the second set. It was, he remembers, "a total difference from being in Nigeria with all my people to being in England on stage with ten white men and four thousand white people in the audience. Myself and Speedy Acquaye were the only Africans. . . . It was the biggest night of my entire career so far, just the one night that I left the stage and didn't remember anything that happened."

The one-year sojourn in England inspired Haastrup to experiment with new songwriting ideas. It was during this period that he composed "Give a Beggar a Chance"—based on observations from his youth when poor people would come to beg money from the owa—and a song called "Lidalu" written for Ginger Baker's daughter. When Airforce broke up in 1971, Haastrup returned home with new sounds in his head and new material in hand.

Back in Lagos he teamed up with bassist Kenneth Okulolo, guitar player Jimmy Lee Adams, and percussionists Candido Obajimi and Friday Jumbo to form a band called Monomono ("lightening"). The new group shunned cover versions of imported hits and concentrated instead on developing an afro-rock sound based on original compositions. It was in constant demand for dances and nightclub performances and in 1972 recorded an album, *Give a Beggar a Chance*, which was an instant hit. A second album, *Dawn of Awareness*, scored favorable comment from *Cashbox* and *Billboard* and was picked up by Capitol Records.

Success fell short of financial reward, however. Record companies were loath to pay royalties to the musicians who were creating their profits. Haastrup recalls having to make threats in order to get paid. "We would have to go in there with the roadies and get into the office looking real wild and say, 'I want some money!'" He feels he was never fully paid what was due the band.

Another source of irritation was the lack of modern recording equipment. Lagos studios were small two- and four-track installations that paled in comparison to state-of-the-art facilities Haastrup had seen in London. He and Fela and others campaigned long and hard to convince EMI to upgrade, but Haastrup recalls that it wasn't until 1973 when Paul McCartney decided to record *Band on the Run* in Lagos that the company agreed. "They wouldn't hear us when we cried for this thing, and we were the people that were there to make the money for them," he says bitterly. "But they would do it because their own person was coming." This may have been a coincidence, however. In his unauthorized biography of Paul McCartney, Chet Flippo reports that McCartney set out for Lagos with little planning and found the EMI studio in the midst of renovation work when he arrived.[3]

In 1975 with Monomono riding high and *Dawn of Awareness* being distributed by Capitol Records, Haastrup traveled to the United States to persuade the company to organize a promotional tour for the band. But Capitol refused, and he returned home. "I went back pretty disgusted," he recalls. "I thought it was all gonna be easy, you know. Because before you came to America it's like everything is pretty easy here. And then when you got here you found that money didn't grow on the streets."

The rejection seemed to demoralize the band, and when Haastrup's second visit to the United States in 1976 again failed to garner support for a tour, Monomono broke up. He returned to Lagos briefly to record a solo album for Decca called *Wake Up Your Mind,* but for most of the rest of the decade he labored as a record producer and session musician in England and America.

The 1980s found Haastrup in northern California, where he jammed with members of the Bay Area's burgeoning community of African musicians. He put together bands of varying style and composition, working with Africans when he could and training Americans to play his music when he had to. But for American musicians, he says, "the rhythm was always the problem. You see, we're all rhythm. So in order to play my music or O.J. or any African, you know, you have to be in rhythm, which is really hard especially for the American musicians. Because even though jazz and soul and all those music have rhythm, still when it comes to the real complex rhythm, I mean even the highlife rhythm which is like a straight 4/4 beat is very hard for the average American musician to comprehend. They just have no clue what it means. I mean, you know, if the one is not on the first beat they couldn't deal with it."

Along the way he abandoned the sometime Christianity and traditional Yoruba religion of his youth to convert to the Nichiren Shoshu sect of Buddhism. "I was attracted to it first of all because it's an all-people philosophy," he explains. "It's a philosophy that anybody can practice, no class difference, no racial difference, no color difference, nothing. . . . It takes me out of the limitation of just wanting to be what people want me to be. It's taken me out into the world of my own where I just want to be what I am. I just want to play my music and make people smile, keep people happy. Not limit myself to what people think I should be."

His goal these days is to come up with the ingredients to penetrate the American market. "I think the only problem with the American music market is that everything, including food, is programmed on TV or radio," he complains. "Everything here is programmed. If you go into Europe as a musician coming out of Africa or coming out of America, you are immediately accepted because they are curious to know what you have that is different. And if you have something good, they go with you. In England, in the continent, they go with you. But in America, the only obvious reason that I can see is that as long as you don't sound like what the Top Forty is playing on the radio, there is not enough open mind to listen to what else there could be."

What galls Haastrup even more is that when established pop artists incorporate elements of African music into their own works, they are praised for their innovation and daring. "Police and, what's the name of Brian Eno's group, you know, all these other bands are making money with the same [African] music," he continues. "When Sunny Ade came here, a bunch of musicians went in and taped his live performance, and now you hear elements of juju music on pop radio. But it's not performed as Sunny Ade would perform it, but it's making millions of dollars. Just because the same thing is taken and rerendered in a more understandable and simpler form. We also know the simple forms, so it's better for us as [African] musicians, as artists who have been in the minority, to start looking at why are we going to continue to remain in the minority."

Haastrup makes the case for his crossover approach. He and many of his contemporaries feel that to break into Western markets they must live and work in those markets; they must adapt and change their music to more closely fit the Top Forty mold. According to this philosophy, failure to adapt is a form of self-denial. Haastrup wants to "show the African musician as an artist first, then as an African. . . . We can be pop, we can be rock, we can be jazz, we can be soul, we can be everything because in actual fact we have [made] an incredible contribution to all of that already. So why deny ourselves, or why deny us, the opportunity to cross over into the commercial industry."

But it's tough to challenge Michael Jackson and Madonna. It's one thing to be a star in Africa and come on tour with a measure of fame and foreign mystique. It's quite another to set up shop in California or New York and find yourself competing for club dates with local garage bands. Even for an American the odds against getting a break in the entertainment industry are staggering. Haastrup says, "My goal is to have one of the really most dynamic groups to ever come out from an African artist. And that's my goal. Because that way people can look at me as an artist, not just as an African." It is an ambitious undertaking—one whose fate is in the hands of a fickle music industry.

An African Musician

Fela Anikulapo-Kuti

13

It's nearly 3 A.M. when Fela Anikulapo-Kuti wanders into the lobby of Baltimore's Lombard Street Holiday Inn. Nigeria's tuneful paragon of provocation hasn't seen a bed for two days. Just after midnight, nearly fifty hours before, his Egypt 80 band had kicked off a concert at Boys and Girls High School in the Bedford-Stuyvesant section of Brooklyn. Unencumbered by curfews, the songs and sermonizing ran on for more than three hours, the kind of gig Fela loves. A thousand miles and three concerts later, he switched the air conditioner in his tenth-floor room over to heat, stripped off his turquoise and white stage costume, and crawled wearily into bed.

In the hotel room's dimness Fela looks much older than he appears onstage. Perhaps it's the rigorous touring schedule, but the lean, lithe body that hours earlier stalked like a drill sergeant about the stage at Wolf Trap outside Washington, D.C., seems frail and fragile away from the paraphernalia of show business. His slender frame is slightly crooked, his brown skin scarred, from sporadic encounters with the truncheons of Nigerian soldiers and police. A splotch of gray hair lies near a bare spot on the back of his head. Settling between the covers as he answers interview questions, Fela fumbles with a cigarette, often showering the bed with fiery ashes as he gestures to make a point.

This is Fela's third American tour since his April 1986 release from a Nigerian prison where he served nearly nineteen months for purportedly violating that country's currency regulations—charges that are widely believed to be false. But for the man who became Africa's second most famous political prisoner after Nelson Mandela, the esteem and adulation that were his in 1986 have considerably dwindled. These days record deals are harder to come by,

and critics of his earnest—some say arrogant—demeanor and pro-
tracted musical excursions are multiplying.

Fela's music is naturally a reflection of his own experience, but
ultimately it mirrors the musical innovations of Africa's descendants throughout the world. From Abeokuta, his birthplace in
southwestern Nigeria, come the rhythms of his Yoruba culture.
The buoyant riffs and rubatos stem from his early love for jazz, the
earthy sensuality from his fascination with the funky soulfulness of
James Brown and Otis Redding.

From his father, the Right Reverend Israel Oludotun Ransome-
Kuti, comes self-righteousness and an artistic discipline along with
the Christian name Ransome, bestowed on Fela's grandfather by
missionaries, which Fela rejected in favor of the Yoruba *Anikulapo,*
"having control over death." Rebelliousness and contempt for
mindless authority spring from Funmilayo, his mother, a pioneer
in Nigeria's movement to expand women's rights. His outrage and
sense of mission seethe from an awareness of his continent's desper-
ate condition—a condition, according to Fela, brought about by
African leaders and their slave-trading, colonizing mentors from
Europe and America.

To Fela's way of thinking, history is repeating itself. Today's African leaders, he says, are just here as "a cause for revelation." Fortified by a long drag on his cigarette, he expands the thought. "You
see, here's what happened. In the fifteenth century, at the beginning
of the slave trade it was the African gods and the European gods
that conspired together to make the slave trade successful. So those
African gods have to replay their parts again for people to see. You
see? So all those leaders in Africa [today] are those [ancient] gods
that have come back to replay those parts that they played in those
times to make Africa what it is today. So that is why they're completely senseless, completely unprogressive, and have to just keep
doing those things that they are doing. . . . I'm here to replay my
part. Everyone's here to replay his part."[1]

This insight came to Fela during a trance in 1981. Through it
and continuing meditation and study, especially with Ghanaian
mystic Professor Hindu, he says he came to understand his part.
"As a matter of fact," he explains, "I was absent during the slave
trade, but I was present in the beginning, in Egypt. . . . I was
Amen Ra Heru Kuti. That was my part. That was who I was in my

Fela Anikulapo-Kuti. Photo © Emmanuel Nado

first presence in this world. So my part was to start Egypt, which I did. Which Isis [an ancient Egyptian goddess], by trickery, took over from me. I had to leave Isis to keep the world running, to show her evil for millions of years before I had to come back now to set things straight. That's my part. Set things straight, say the truth about what's happening without fear and let the progress go on."

"Music is the weapon," Fela likes to say, and setting things straight takes a lot of it. He is famous—some would say infamous—for songs that run on nearly half an hour or more. "When I have to say so much, I cannot say it in a short time. . . . My songs are now even getting much longer." He tells how he explained it to representatives of Polygram who had expressed an interest in signing him for their label: "You cannot class my music like American music, because, I said, my music is in different movements. You have to class it by movements, so you cannot say Fela is writing one song. No! Fela is writing a song with five movements. . . . It's like a symphony but in the African sense."

The symphonic analogy is equally apt for describing Fela's orchestra, Egypt 80. The size of the troupe hovers around thirty, including a dozen singers and dancers, a nine-member brass section, two basses, two guitars, trap drums, keyboards, various African percussion instruments, and Fela on his own keyboard and saxophone. "To play African music you cannot economize," he says. "The culture of Africa is not based on economy, it's based on naturalness, being natural. And if you try to put money first before the culture, then you will destroy the beauty of what you wanted to represent. And I don't have any intention to destroy the beauty of African music for money. I will never do that. So I'm the poorest musician in town right now."

Fela's musical acuity preceded his understanding of the political and spiritual worlds by several years. As a teenager in the 1950s he played with friends in a pickup band and sang occasionally with Victor Olaiya's highlife group. In 1958 he went off to London to play trumpet and study European classical music at Trinity College of Music, but outside class what captured Fela's attention was jazz.

After four and a half years abroad, he returned home with a dream. "My intention was to introduce jazz into Nigeria when I first came," he recalls. "And I had this quartet, Fela Ransome-Kuti Quartet, trumpet, guitar, drums, and bass. But I was so unsuccessful. People just refused to accept it." Fela persisted for a time, but he remembers that when a free concert failed to attract a crowd, "that one discouraged me completely."

He began to incorporate African rhythms into his jazz compositions, essentially repeating what had happened with the birth of highlife in Ghana several decades earlier. Joni Haastrup remembers that "it was like jazz highlife fusion. And people couldn't relate to it because he had all these horns and all these arrangements, and it was all too much for the people to comprehend. . . . He was playing to empty houses while we were packing [them]."[2]

By the midsixties Fela and nearly every other African musician began to feel the heat of new competition from the West. "Soul music took over," he says. "James Brown's music, Otis Redding, took over the whole continent, man. It was beautiful music though, I must agree. I said to myself I must compete with these people. I must find a name for my music, so I gave my music [the name] *afro-beat* to give it an identity. . . . But you see it did not work, because I had not played Africa. I had not played the music of Africa. It was in '69 when I came to America that I knew where my fault was. I had not even known any history of my continent. I had not really investigated, I had not really made myself a part of my continent. So when I went back home in '70, I decided to study real African music, which brought the new sound of what people started to know [as afro-beat]."

Koola Lobitos, a name Fela now calls meaningless that was coined for his London group and adopted again when he began playing highlife and afro-beat, was changed on his return from American to Africa 70. To Fela's way of thinking, Africa 70 meant something; it looked to the future and heralded a new musical and political direction. He also abandoned his trumpet in favor of the tenor sax, which he found to be easier on the lips.

Fela's restless, brooding new synthesis of African musical elements coupled with militant, biting social commentary was explosive. Nigeria's masses embraced it while their rulers reacted with alarm. Albums like *Alagbon Close* and *Expensive Shit* depicted Fela's brushes with the law; others such as *V.I.P. Vagabonds in Power* and *Authority Stealing* were searing indictments of the Nigerian power structure.

Needless to say the authorities did not take kindly to such a bar-
rage of criticism. Fela was often harassed. His Lagos residence, the
self-proclaimed Kalakuta Republic, was sacked by the army in
1977; a 1979 run for the presidency stalled when his Movement of
the People was denied recognition as a political party by electoral
officials; and more recently he served time on the suspect currency
rap.

These days, his political aspirations are "inclined in the spiritual
sense." "Now I know I will rule my country," he says. "I know that.
Whether I want to do it through politics or through spiritual
means is what I have to decide myself. You see I'm still trying to
balance and decipher what exactly should happen in my country."

When Fela talks African politics, his sense of outrage and disgust
is unmistakable. His voice assumes a cynical, almost sneering tone
as he derides African rulers who emulate their colonial pre-
decessors. "You cannot control African people with white man's
laws; you have to make your own laws for your own people," he
exclaims. "The more they still want to do it the white man's way, the
more corrupt it goes. . . . They have succeeded to make white
man's knowledge *the* knowledge. So when you are a professor you
have a say in society. Ah ha! That's a problem. So everybody wants
to be professor; everybody wants to be Alhaji, everybody wants to
be [shrugs]. You know? So they've really managed to brainwash
people into thinking these are the best things. And it's so retrogressive."

But on some issues Fela too can sound retrogressive. While he
ranks high as a champion of the downtrodden masses, his professed
attitude toward women seems strangely unenlightened in this era
of increasing awareness of sexism's pernicious effects. He once had
twenty-eight wives, twenty-seven of whom he married all at once.
The song "Mattress," which describes his vision of woman's earthly
purpose, to satisfy her man, and "Lady," a satire about women with
the temerity to claim equality with men, are graphic statements of
his feelings toward the world's majority gender.

Such statements Fela is loath to recant. "To call me a sexist . . . for me it's still not a negative name," he says. "If I'm a sexist,
it's a gift. Not everybody can fuck two women every day. So if I can
fuck two women every day and they [critics] don't like it, I'm sorry

for them. I just like it. It's sweet. I mean sex is essence. . . . The Creator is in permanent essence, and he has given the human beings the opportunity to experience that essence when they have sex. So why should you run away from it? Why should you give it a bad name when it's what the Creator experiences permanently?"

Between male and female, he continues, "Sex is mutual. But when it comes to who is culturally superior in society, that is also dictated by nature according to the African sense. The Africans believe that women have their natural duties, and men have their natural duties, and both of them cannot contradict, or both of them do not have contradictions, and they are not supposed to challenge each other. . . . I'm not saying don't be feminist if you want to be in Europe, but I tell you in Africa the women will not even try to be feminists."

Today Fela has no wives and no longer believes in marriage. "In prison [1984–1986] I was able to really meditate and go deeper into my spiritual life," he explains, "and I found out marriage was not a natural concept; it was an institution. On any level, even in the African cultural sense, in any cultural sense, it was an institution. . . . What is marriage? Why is it necessary to marry if two of you want to have children and live together? You see? Then I saw the African concept of marriage as not really being married because you could leave your husband any time you wanted to, or you could sack your wife any time you wanted to; okay, that's quite reasonable. But then why do you have to go through the exercise anyway?" He calls marriage "retrogressive," saying that men and women are often attracted to people other than their mates. "Marriage is negating a natural human feeling. . . . So having children should be dealt with on a much higher level."

If in his analysis of sex roles Fela remains immutable, his spiritual awakening during the last decade has brought about changes. "In my trance," he says, "the spirits made me understand that I have to make people understand that Egyptian civilization was purely African and that the concept of civilization being stolen from Africans by the Greeks, by the Arabs, should be negated by my preachings and my songs and my outbursts. So the first thing to do was to change my band to Egypt 80 so to make people, Africans, realize that Egyptian civilization was African."

He doesn't play afro-beat anymore, he explains. "I've gone into more serious kind of thing now. . . . I don't want to make African music a fashion. I just want people to know African music as African music, full stop, because African music is so diverse. So to call it afro-beat is retrogressive in a way if it's gonna be serious. So I decided to call my music African music for people to see where I was going. Understand? Because I'm not really writing music based on my area, I'm writing music on the whole of Africa."

His primary inspiration comes from traditional sources. He largely disdains contemporary pop music. "Okay, I may listen to it to see what's happening," he says, "but I still prefer to listen to deep sounds from the villages all over Africa. That's where I get a lot of rhythms, spiritualness, from there, you know." A quote from former South African president P. W. Botha triggered "Beasts of No Nation"; an unusual rhythm heard outside his prison cell in Maiduguri became the foundation for "Pansa Pansa."

When writing his songs, Fela usually begins with the bass. "Sometimes I start with just the rhythmical pattern, few times. A couple of three or four times I've started with the guitar. But I never start with melody. I take it the other way round. But most of the times it's from the bass line. I hear the bass; I know what to put into the bass; I put guitar; I put rhythm; then I put the horns. Then I get the bad sound. Then I go home and write the song. I write the words first, then I write the tune [melody]." He writes out the horn charts, but the rest of the players get only verbal instruction.

Live performance becomes the showcase for new material. Once a song has been recorded, Fela never again performs it in concert. "If you want to hear 'Zombie' go buy the record; I like to move forward," he once told a concertgoer who shouted a request. "You see for me, I don't believe in falling on old tunes to play to the audience," he explains. "I want my audience to feel me where I'm at, not where I was. To feel me where I'm at gives me progress, makes me feel I am communicating. So to fall back and start to play old tunes, for me it's retrogressive. It doesn't give me the challenge and impetus to write new songs. You see? With that kind of decision I'm forced to write, keep writing."

Finding sources of inspiration and composing songs are the easy parts. Getting the music recorded and distributed is becoming

more difficult. Economic decline is extracting a heavy toll in
Nigeria. Because of currency devaluations it is nearly impossible
for musicians to afford instruments. Recording studios have begun
to deteriorate as foreign currency to purchase improvements from
abroad becomes increasingly scarce. Decca and EMI have twenty-
four track studios, and there are a few with eight or sixteen tracks.
"But," says Fela, "studios are so terrible. They're not what's happening today. So that when we make records at home, [we] cannot
push [them] internationally because of the quality." Basic tracks for
Beasts of No Nation were laid in Lagos then overdubbed and mixed
in Paris. A later album, *Overtake Don Overtake Overtake,* was recorded in London.

If recording is a problem, gaining international distribution is
even more of a struggle. For whatever reason, be it musical or financial, the only European record company willing to release Fela's
work is the small French label Justine. Across the Atlantic,
Shanachie, the independent New Jersey label that helped to introduce African and Caribbean music in the United States, is
seemingly the only company willing to deal with him at the moment.

But if Fela is nothing else, he is confident. He has faith in himself
and in his music. "I know exactly what I'm doing in this world
now," he exclaims. He feels everything has its time. "I cannot tell
you it's gonna take this, gonna take that, before African music
breaks into America, into the world. You know? It will break into
the world, but it will take its time, very gradually but very system-
atic and consistent, because that is the best way for the music to
break. The gods do not want the music to break into the international scene as a fashion. It wants it to break in as a serious cultural
episode."

According to Fela, the wrong African music is being pushed in
Europe and America. He believes most African artists are presented as curiosities by unscrupulous and unknowledgeable promoters who care more for the money than the music. "Those kinds
of things destroy the concept of what the gods want it to be," he
says. "As time goes on, people will start to realize the importance,
the effect, and the seriousness, the intricacies, the beauty, and the
spiritual purpose of the music."

After fifty-two years in this life, more than thirty of which he has spent entertaining, educating, and enraging various constituencies, Fela seems to be at peace with himself. His spiritual awakening has led him to believe that he is on the side of destiny. He is certain that he and his music have a worthy purpose, which in time the larger world will come to understand.

Politics and Papa's Land

Sonny Okosuns

14

A television host once called him "the hot potato kid." An early press account spoke of "the kid with the king-size ambition." Both were describing Nigeria's Sonny Okosuns, today no longer a kid but still ambitious and definitely hot. Backed by his masterful Ozziddi band, Okosuns is a musical militant, a saber-tongued warrior in the fight for African justice.

On records he sings of "Fire in Soweto" and asks "Which Way Nigeria?" Onstage he's a fountain of pent-up energy exploding in fits and starts, dancing, prancing, snatching the microphone to scream another chorus. He plays an eclectic mix of reggae and afro-soul and sings not of romance and infatuation but of freedom and liberation. To sing about love "is really very, very cheap, because it's more commercial," Okosuns says. "I would like to leave a very nice document, you know, behind. I would like people to think about it. I would like to be useful to the society."[1]

That's quite a turnaround for a man who grew up admiring the music of Elvis Presley, Cliff Richard, and the Beatles. His first group, formed in 1965 in the old Eastern Region capital Enugu, was in fact a Beatles imitation called the Postmen. "Our clothes and our hair like the Beatles," he says. "We were just singing Beatles songs then." When American soul music swept Nigeria in the mid-sixties, the Heartbeats and the Clusters captured Lagos with their James Brown routines. Even highlife bands had to play "copyright" music to keep their audiences.

But Okosuns's musical roots extend beyond the fads of Western pop music. His parents were both traditional musicians, and young Sonny was exposed to the songs and rhythms of eastern Nigeria from the day of his birth in 1947. Growing up in Enugu, Okosuns—who incidentally likes the *s* that has been inadvertently hung on his original Okosun and now uses it himself—came of age in the highlife era when Victor Olaiya, Rex Lawson, Bobby Benson, and a host of other Nigerian highlife bands ruled the entertainment scene.

He entertained fantasies of becoming an actor and moving to Hollywood, but his father wanted him to be an automobile engineer. "I wanted it too," he remembers, "but I just didn't like mathematics at all." Instead, he learned to play guitar from a friend and began to study acting with a theater group called the Villagers. In 1965 he traveled to London as a member of the Eastern Nigeria Theater Group when the troupe represented Nigeria at the Commonwealth Arts Festival.

When Nigeria's civil war broke out in 1967, Okosuns and his family fled west to Lagos to escape the fighting. There, through connections made at the Commonwealth Arts Festival, he landed a job with Nigerian television where he worked as a stagehand and graphic artist and occasionally filled in for on-air talent.

As we saw earlier, Nigeria's civil war seriously affected the music scene. Highlife bands, which generally tended to reflect the country's diverse ethnic mixture, suddenly lost their Igbo members, who retreated to the east. Bandleaders like Rex Lawson and Celestine Ukwu and Zeal Onyia, all easterners, left Lagos at the war's onset. Okosuns recalls that entire pop groups like the Attractions and the Fractions all fled to the east. Western bandleaders such as Victor Olaiya, Bobby Benson, and Roy Chicago remained in Lagos, but nightlife was radically curtailed by blackouts and the ranks of musicians thinned by conscription.

Around 1969 Okosuns began to play with Victor Uwaifo, who was riding the crest of his "Joromi" and "Guitar Boy" fame. They did a European tour and in 1970 performed in Japan. Meanwhile, the war had ended with the defeat of secessionist Biafra in January 1970, and the country was slowly returning to normal. On his return from Japan, Okosuns decided to strike out on his own.

As the new decade dawned, the music scene began to shift. Fela returned from America to put more African elements into his afrobeat. Haastrup brought new ideas from London after his stint with Ginger Baker's Airforce. Among young Nigerians, it was the era of underground music, of Jimi Hendrix and Traffic. "If you weren't a part of it," Okosuns remembers, "you weren't a part of the youth."

Paperback Limited, his new group, appealed to younger audiences, but he wanted to play his own music, which posed a dilemma. "I got all the youth, you know, who were so much interested in underground, but I lost them when they started listening to the kind of music I was playing. I wasn't playing the . . . Jimi Hendrix kind of music or the Who or the Kinks kind of music. . . . That's what the youth wanted to hear."

He swung back and forth, playing his own music then switching to "copyright," trying to find an audience. "You see," he says, "I was in the crossroads. I was winning one way but losing in many ways." By constantly changing he was failing to satisfy anyone, but the experiment had a benefit. Okosuns began to see more clearly what he wanted to do: "If I had to be a professional musician, I must have a message." He dissolved Paperback Limited in 1974 and regrouped with a new band he called Ozziddi.

Okosuns remembers first thinking of the name when he read a play called *Ozidi,* by Nigerian author John Pepper Clark, whose main character was a god of the Ijaw people.[2] He also recalled a similar phrase from the Igbo language, *ozi di* (there is a message). He combined the two to define his musical mission; for Okosuns, Ozziddi means simply "there is a message."

His first big hit with the new group was a reggae number called "Help." The strong cultural ties between Jamaica and West Africa make reggae a favorite along the former Slave Coast. Later songs like "Fire in Soweto" and "Holy Wars" set to the slow, rolling reggae rhythm carried the Ozziddi sound far beyond the borders of Nigeria. Reggae's stars began to take notice. Okosuns did Nigerian tours with Jimmy Cliff and Toots and the Maytals. When Peter Tosh was writing the songs for *Mama Africa,* he stayed with Okosuns in Lagos. Okosuns says Bob Marley once wrote to him to say he planned to record "Holy Wars."

"Reggae gives you space to write the kind of lyrics, protest lyrics especially, that we like to write," he says. "But I still very much love the hard African song. We trained ourself to be able to write some hard protest songs into African songs like 'Papa's Land' and 'Tell Them' too." In fact Okosuns plays a variety of styles. His convulsive afro-soul features punchy James Brown–style horns and a hard-rocking rhythm section. He did an album with calypsonian Lord

Sonny Okosuns

Superior and has worked with Mighty Sparrow and Eddy Grant. "I must say," he continues, "that I've learnt from the past experience from other people that when you are stuck to one kind of beat and when that beat fades, then you fade along with it. You see, to be a real good musician, you should be able to touch a lot of things."

The basic Ozziddi lineup includes trumpet, trombone, keyboards, guitar, bass, trap drums, and congas. Okosuns often takes up a small talking drum or other percussion piece to enhance the rhythmic mix. Three female backup singers shimmy and shake as they harmonize behind Okosuns's lead vocal. It's a versatile combination capable of finessing a rootsy "Rain" and blitzing a hard, biting "Tell Them" with equal skill.

Whatever the genre, Okosuns writes all his own material. He often uses song titles to trigger ideas. "A title just flashes through my mind, or I see it somewhere," he explains. "For instance 'Journey to the Congo.' You know, how would that one make a sense? That would take me many weeks to think about, you know. Does it really make a sense? Maybe I start interacting with people, say, 'Oh! Journey to Africa, Journey to So and So,' you know, that kind of thing. Then if I have to stick to that title it means I must have a particular audience that I'm directing that song to. 'Man on the Run.' Why should it be 'Man on the Run?' Why? Who is this man on the run? You know, that kind of thing. Then I have to write. Or sometimes I get a tune, you know melody, and start humming it. Like 'Rain' . . . for six months I didn't get lyrics to it. I didn't get lyrics that would suit it until one day I was just sitting down and it started raining, you know. And I said, what about rain? You know? Then I went in and started writing."

He once entertained the idea of writing new words and melodies for the Beatles catalog of titles—"Help" was a first attempt—but gave up because so many suggested love. "I didn't want to go into love singing at all," he says. "I wanted to sing something meaningful, protest songs." Aiming beyond narrow ethnic and national boundaries, he always writes in English because "it will be easier for people to understand instead of after singing just asking questions. If I had sang all my songs in vernacular, you know, you'll only just come in and dance to the rhythm, that's all, without hearing one word of what I'm saying."

What he is saying has drawn praise from across the African continent. Heads of state as philosophically opposite as the revered Thomas Sankara of Burkina Faso and the hated Samuel Doe of Liberia rallied their people to the sounds of Sonny Okosuns. In Nigeria itself, politicians often have appropriated his messages to further their own causes. "When I did 'Power to the People' [in 1979], I was actually asking the federal [military] government of Obasanjo then, that they should hand power over to the people. . . . Then Zik's [Nnamdi Azikiwe's] party, which is Nigerian People's Party or something like that, adopted that slogan 'power to the people.' So when it was released, ah! everybody said, 'Aha! Sonny Okosuns, you sang a song for Zik, why don't you sing a song for Shagari or sing for Awolowo?'"

During the election campaign of 1983, Okosuns released "Togetherness." "The national television used that one as a slogan to bring the people together," he continues. "And people said I used it for, I mean it was to please Shagari, because Shagari was going to win." In the event, President Shehu Shagari did win reelection.

Okosuns then wrote and recorded "Which Way Nigeria" in, of all places, New York. "When I released it," he says, "the whole radio stations refused to play it. They said I was directing the song to, you know, to Shagari and his government." When three months after the start of his second term Shagari was overthrown by the military, "Which Way Nigeria" suddenly found favor, "and the Minister of Information then used that record as a slogan [to explain] why they took over the government."

Outside Africa Okosuns's lyrics are controversial for another reason: Record company executives feel they are not commercial. He has refused requests to change his songs for the American market. It is a difficult stand to take when one considers the widespread distribution and potential profit a major record company can offer. But for the present at least, Okosuns remains true to his principles: "I need a record company that will take my music the way it is."

Despite the lure of Europe and America and a deteriorating economy at home—twin incentives that have caused so many of his contemporaries to move abroad—Okosuns prefers to live and work in Nigeria. "I think it's the comfort we enjoy at home and the reception and the acceptance we enjoy at home," he explains. "We were actually trained not to leave our responsibilities at home and just go and start searching for greener pastures, come and live in New York. For instance if we had come to live here, I don't think we would really be taken seriously the way we are taken seriously now. . . . I know so many of my friends that came here and lost touch with home. Now they can't come back home to start all over again. If they come now, they will start from where they left."

But if international success springs from a popular base of support at home, it also requires the massive doses of exposure and promotion that record companies lavish on their rock stars. "Right now it's still not what it should be," Okosuns complains. "The way we accepted Western music is not the way we're being accepted right now. I know about three or four years ago they took it as novelty. Everybody was just watching to know what kind of primitive music that we'll come with from Africa with Western instruments and so on and so forth. But I don't think that is the way it is now. . . . We need one, a very good recording company, okay, like what Island Records did to reggae, Bob Marley and reggae and all those things. We need a recording company that will really stand up and say . . . okay, we're going to promote African music in America or in Europe."

If such an event is to happen, Okosuns plans to be there. It happened for him in Nigeria; now he has set his sights on the West. "You just have to work hard to be original," he says. "And with luck, if you break through with two or three songs, man, then you are there. Then your sound has arrived."

Notes

Introduction

1. John Storm Roberts, *Black Music of Two Worlds* (New York: Praeger Publishers, 1972), 40.

2. Iain Lang, "Jazz Comes Home to Africa," *West African Review,* December 1956, 1088.

3. Joni Haastrup; all quotations in this chapter from interview with author, Oakland, California, 11 February 1986.

4. Sonny Okosuns, interview with author, Toronto, Ontario, 3 June 1989.

5. Ibrahim Bah, telephone interview with author, 15 November 1986.

6. Stewart Levine, telephone interview with author, 16 January 1990.

One: Soukous Chic

1. Kanda Bongo Man; unless otherwise noted, all quotations in this chapter from interview with author, Toronto, Ontario, 12 May 1989.

2. James Marck, "Kanda's Zaire Soukous Sound," *NOW* (Toronto), 11–17 May 1989, 23.

3. Joe Boyd; all quotations in this chapter from telephone interview with author, 6 June 1989.

4. Diblo Dibala; all quotations in this chapter from interview with author, Washington, D.C., 28 September 1989.

Two: God of the Guitar

1. Docteur Nico; all quotations in this chapter from interview with author, Washington, D.C., 20 and 22 March 1985.

2. Roberts, *Black Music of Two Worlds,* 245.

3. Tabu Ley Rochereau; all quotations in this chapter from interview with author, Arlington, Virginia, 8 October 1989.

4. Isaac Musekiwa; all quotations in this chapter from interview with author, Washington, D.C., and Arlington, Virginia, 3 August 1989.

5. Quoted in Richard D. Mahoney, *JFK: Ordeal in Africa* (New York: Oxford University Press, 1983), 39.

6. Ibid., 40–41, 52–53, 66–74.

7. For an account of Mobutu's authenticity campaign see Victor D. Du

Bois, "Zaire under President Sese Seko Mobutu, Part 1: The Return to Authenticity," *AUFS Fieldstaff Reports,* Central and Southern Africa Series, vol. 27, no. 1 (Hanover: American Universities Field Staff, 1973).

Three: Toujours O.K.

1. Sam Mangwana says that although Franco and his band failed to show up for the scheduled concert, it was visa problems and not Franco's health that prevented the performance. Interview with author, Washington, D.C., 15 October 1990.

2. Nsala Manzenza and Dizzy Mandjeku; all information and quotations in this chapter from interview with author, Washington, D.C., 3 August 1989.

3. Philippe Conrath, "Franco, la rumba à mort," *Libération* (Paris), 16 October 1989, 46.

4. Dessouin Bosuma, interview with author, Washington, D.C., and Arlington, Virginia, 3 August 1989.

5. *Franco and his T.P.O.K. Jazz in U.S.A.,* program for U.S. tour November–December 1983, 4.

6. Jean-Jacques Kande, quoted in Michel Lonoh, *Essai de commentaire sur la musique Congolaise moderne* (Kinshasa: St. Paul, 1969), 124.

7. Ibid., 126.

8. Isaac Musekiwa, interview with author, Washington, D.C., 3 August 1989.

9. Gerry Dialungana, interview with author, Washington, D.C., 3 August 1989.

10. Jon Pareles, "The Pop Life," *New York Times,* 30 November 1983, C26.

11. Ibrahim Bah, interview with author, Washington, D.C., 25 November 1984.

12. "Franco: Last Days in London," *Tradewind: Stern's Music Review* (London) 2, no. 11 (November 1989): 3.

Four: Ubongo Man

1. For more about the benga beat of Kenya see Chris Stapleton and Chris May, *African All-Stars* (London: Quartet Books, 1987), 230–34.

2. Remmy Ongala; because a malfunctioning tape recorder refused to record an interview with Ongala, all quotations in this chapter are taken from the author's interview notes and from Ongala's press conference held in Toronto, Ontario, 13 August 1989.

3. Roger Wallis and Krister Malm, *Big Sounds from Small Peoples* (London: Constable, 1984), 152, 237.

4. Ibid., 260.

Five: The Palm Wine Picker

1. S. E. Rogie; all quotations in this chapter, unless otherwise noted, from interviews with author, El Sobrante and Richmond, California, April 1984 and 21 May 1986.

2. Information from producer and radio personality Chris During, interview with author, Freetown, Sierra Leone, 26 January 1989.

3. Valerie Wilmer, "S. E. Rogers' Life Story," in *Rogie International Song Book*, compiled by S.E. Rogers (Freetown, Sierra Leone: S. E. Rogers, 1970), 6.

4. Ibid., 7.

5. Sarah Coxson, "The Song of Sooliman," *Folk Roots* 59 (May 1988): 17.

6. Wilmer, "S. E. Rogers' Life Story," 10.

Six: A Vanishing Breed

1. Big Fayia; all quotations in this chapter from interview with author, Freetown, Sierra Leone, 4 January 1987.

2. Chris During; all quotations in this chapter from interview with author, Freetown, Sierra Leone, 26 January 1989.

Seven: Graceland's Heartbeat

1. Francis Fuster; all quotations in this chapter from interview with author, London, 12 March 1989.

2. Chris During; all quotations in this chapter from interview with author, Freetown, Sierra Leone, 26 January 1989.

3. Naomi Ware, "Popular Music and African Identity in Freetown, Sierra Leone," in *Eight Urban Musical Cultures: Tradition and Change,* ed. Bruno Nettl (Urbana: University of Illinois Press, 1978), 303.

4. Fela Anikulapo-Kuti, interview with author, Baltimore, Maryland, 6 July 1990.

Eight: Dance the Highlife

1. John Collins, *E. T. Mensah: King of Highlife* (London: Off The Record Press, 1986), 10.

2. David Coplan, "Go to My Town, Cape Coast! The Social History of Ghanaian Highlife," in *Eight Urban Musical Cultures: Tradition and Change*, ed. Bruno Nettl (Urbana: University of Illinois Press, 1978), 100–102.

3. Nana Ampadu; all quotations in this chapter from interview with author, Alexandria, Virginia, 19 September 1987.

4. Kwabena N. Bame, *Come to Laugh* (New York: Lillian Barber Press, 1985), 46–47.

5. For more about concert parties see Bame (note 4 above) and also John Collins, *Musicmakers of West Africa* (Washington: Three Continents Press, 1985), 21–32.

6. John Miller Chernoff, "Africa Come Back: The Popular Music of West Africa," in *Repercussions: A Celebration of African-American Music*, ed. Geoffrey Haydon and Dennis Marks (London: Century Publishing, 1985), 167.

Nine: High Times, Hard Times

1. Stewart Levine; all quotations in this chapter from telephone interview with author, 16 January 1990.

2. Okyerema Asante; all quotations in this chapter from interview with author, Springfield, Virginia, 3 January 1990.

3. Acheampong "Salas" Welbeck; all quotations in this chapter from interviews with author, Berkeley and Oakland, California, 21 March, 19 April, and 20 July 1986.

4. Paajoe Amissah; all quotations in this chapter from interviews with author, Berkeley and Oakland, California, 21 March, 19 April, and 20 July 1986.

5. Fela Anikulapo-Kuti, interview with author, Baltimore, Maryland, 6 July 1990.

6. Arlynn Nellhaus, "Masekela High on New Sound," *Denver Post*, 30 January 1974, 39.

Ten: The Beat Goes On

1. Mickey Hart; all quotations in this chapter from telephone interview with author, 3 October 1988.

2. Babatunde Olatunji; all quotations in this chapter from interview with author, Oakland, California, 1 August 1987.

3. Chinua Achebe, *Things Fall Apart* (New York: Astor-Honor, 1959).

4. Robert Farris Thompson, from liner notes to *Zungo* by Olatunji (Columbia Records, CL 1634, 1961).

Eleven: The Dawn of Afro-Beat

1. Orlando Julius Ekemode; all quotations in this chapter from interviews with author, Oakland, California, 15 February 1986 and 15 July 1987.

2. "Night Out in Lagos," *West African Review,* June 1959, 482.

3. Albert McKay, "High-Life Boom Hits West Africa," *West African Review,* January 1957, 77.

4. Christopher Alan Waterman, *Juju: A Social History and Ethnography of an African Popular Music* (Chicago: University of Chicago Press, 1990), 90–91.

5. Fela Anikulapo-Kuti, interview with author, Baltimore, Maryland, 6 July 1990.

6. Cyprian Ekwensi, "Nana-Jagua Nana," *West African Review,* August 1957, 791. Ekwensi is also the author of a full-length novel of similar title and subject matter, *Jagua Nana* (London: Hutchinson, 1961).

7. Barry Lee Pearson, *Sounds So Good to Me* (Philadelphia: University of Pennsylvania Press, 1984), 105.

Twelve: Soul Brother Number One

1. Joni Haastrup; all quotations in this chapter from interview with author, Oakland, California, 11 February 1986.

2. Valerie Wilmer, "Ginger Baker: Anglo Afro?" *Down Beat,* 19 March 1970, 17.

3. Chet Flippo, *Yesterday: The Unauthorized Biography of Paul McCartney* (New York: Doubleday, 1988), 331.

Thirteen: An African Musician

1. Fela Anikulapo-Kuti; all quotations in this chapter from interview with author, Baltimore, Maryland, 6 July 1990.

2. Joni Haastrup, interview with author, Oakland, California, 11 February 1986.

Fourteen: Politics and Papa's Land

1. Sonny Okosuns; all quotations in this chapter from interview with author, Toronto, Ontario, 3 June 1989.

2. John Pepper Clark, *Ozidi* (London: Oxford University Press, 1966).

Discography

This discography is a sampling of the works produced by the artists profiled. In cases where albums were released on more than one label, I have tried to list the U.S. issue whenever possible. With a little work, many of these recordings (most are records and tapes but some are now available on compact disc) can still be found. Others are out of print but are included for the sake of historical perspective. Dates given are recording dates as best as can be ascertained rather than release dates, unless accompanied by an *R*. Many thanks to Ibrahim Bah of the African Music Gallery in Washington, D.C., and to *The Beat* magazine's "Africana" columnist Elizabeth Sobo for their assistance in compiling this list.

Kanda Bongo Man

1981	Afro Rythmes	45305-1	*Iyole-Mazina*
1982	Afro Rythmes	45306-1	*Djessy-Dyna*
1984	Bongo Man	BM0055	*Amour Fou-Ekipe*
1985	Bongo Man	BM0056	*Malinga–J.T.*
1986R	Globestyle	ORB005	*Non Stop Non Stop* (compilation of AR45305 & 45306)
1987R	Hannibal	HNBL1337	*Amour Fou/Crazy Love* (compilation of BM0055 and BM0056)
1987	Bongo Man	BM0057	*Lela Lela*
1987	Bongo Man	BM0058	*Sai-Liza*
1989R	Hannibal	HNBL1343	*Kwassa Kwassa* (compilation of BM0057 and BM0058)
1990	Bongo Man	BM0059	*Isambi-Monie*

Docteur Nico
With African Jazz

Late 1950s	African	360.142	*Hommage au Grand Kallé*, vol. 1
and	African	360.143	*Hommage au Grand Kallé*, vol. 2
Early 1960s	African	360.107	*Authenticité*, vol. 5
	Pathé Marconi	C062-15810	*African Memories* (African Jazz, and Rock-A-Mambo, 1976 reissue)

With African Fiesta:

1962–63	African	360.162	*African Fiesta 1962 1963*
1962–63	African	360.163	*African Fiesta 1962 1963*
1963–65	African	360.151	*Eternel Docteur Nico 1963 1965*
1963–65	African	360.152	*Eternel Docteur Nico 1963 1965*
1967	African	360.159	*Eternel Docteur Nico 1967*
1967	African	360.160	*Eternel Docteur Nico 1967*
1969	African	360.005	*L'Afrique Danse*, no. 5 (avec le Docteur Nico et son orchestre)
1969	African	360.011	*L'Afrique Danse*, no. 8

With African Fiesta Sukisa:

1969 or 1970	African	360.020	*L'Afrique Danse*, no. 9
1970	African	360.024	*L'Afrique Danse*, no. 10

Again with African Fiesta:

1975	sonafric	SAF50.003	*Toute L'Afrique Danse*
1975	sonafric	SAF50007	*Docteur Nico et l'Orchestre African Fiesta*

(Copyright date for these two LPs is 1975, but they may be earlier recordings.)

Comeback recordings:

1984	Africa New Sound	ANS8404	*Dieu de la Guitare*, no. 1

1984	Africa New Sound	ANS8412	*Aux USA*
1984	African Music Gallery	AMG008	*Adieu*

Franco and l'Orchestre O.K. Jazz

This list accounts for only a small fraction of Franco's prodigious output. For a more thorough Franco discography, see Graeme Ewens, *Luambo Franco and 30 Years of O.K. Jazz*.

1956–59	RetroAfric	RETRO2	*Originalité*
1960–62	African	360.125	*Authenticité 1960–1962*
1962–63	African	360.078	*Authenticité, vol. 4*
1962–64	African	360.124	*Authenticité 1962–1964*
1963	African	360.156	*Les Merveilles du Passé 1963*
1960s	African	360.070	*Authenticité, vol. 1*
1964–66	African	360.072	*Authenticité, vol. 3*
1960s	African	360.010	*Les Merveilles du Passé, no. 1*
1968	African	360.006	*L'Afrique Danse, no. 6*
1960s	Pathé Marconi	STX 229	*A Paris*
1960s	Pathé Marconi	150 15973/74	*O.K. Jazz, vol. 1 and 2*
1972	Pathé Marconi	062 15574	*Les Grands Succés Africains, vol. 4*
1973	African	360.053	*Editions Populaires*
1974	African	360.056	*Editions Populaires*
1976	African	360.082/083	*20e Anniversaire*
1977	African	360.096	*African Party*
1977	African	360.116	*Live Chez 1-2-3 à Kinshasa*
1978	African	360.114/115	*Live Recording of Afro-European Tour*
1979	African	360.132	*Africain Dances*
1980	Makossa	M2377	*A Paris* (same as Visa 1980 FRAN 001/002)
1980	Visa 1980	FRAN 004/005	*Le 24ème Anniversaire*

1981	Edipop	POP 02	*Bimansha*
1981	Edipop	POP 03	*Le Quart de Siècle Vol. 3 Tailleur*
1982	Edipop	POP 17	*Coopération* (with Sam Mangwana)
1982	Edipop	POP 021	*Disque d'Or et Maracas d'Or*
1983	Edipop	POP 027	*Chez Fabrice à Bruxelles*
1983	Choc Choc Choc	CHOC000/ 001	*De Bruxelles à Paris*, le Grand Maître Franco/le Seigneur Rochereau
1983	Shanachie	43024	*Omona Wapi*, Franco and Rochereau
1984	Edipop	POP 028	*Très Impoli*
1985	Choc Choc Choc	CHOC004	*Mario*
1986 or 1987	Celluloid	9508	*Ekaba-Kaba*
1987	African Sun Music	ASM 001	*Attention na SIDA*
1989	Syllart	SYL8396	*For Ever* with Sam Mangwana
1989	Rythmes et Musique	RMU850	*Joue avec Sam Mangwana*

Remmy Ongala

early 1980s	WOMAD	010	*Nalilia Mwana*
1988R	AHADI	6007	*On Stage with Remmy Ongala*
1989	Real World	91315-1	*Songs for the Poor Man*

S. E. Rogie

1960s	Rogiphone	R2	*The 60s' Sounds of S. E. Rogie*
1960s	Cooking Vinyl	COOK010	*Palm Wine Guitar Music* (same as R2 plus two additional tracks)
1975	Rogiphone	R1	*African Lady*
1979	Highlife	AL-2	*Mother Africa*
1989	Workers Playtime	PLAY LP9	*The Palm Wine Sounds of S. E. Rogie*

| 1991 | Workers Playtime | PLAY CD18 | *The New Sounds of S. E. Rogie,* S. E. Rogie and His Palm Wine Tappers |

Big Fayia

1976	Afrodisc (45)	AD-1006A	*Alay Wu Waa*
1977	DBF (45 rpm)	DBF40	*Want Want No Get*
1977	DBF (45 rpm)	DBF42	*Respect*
1979	J. & H. Samuh (45 rpm)	07SL2	*Looking for a Woman* with the Sierra Leone Military Dance Band
1980	J. & H. Samuh	No number	*QAU 1980* with the Sierra Leone Military Dance Band
1986	Big Fayia (cassette)	No number	*Big Fayia*

Francis Fuster

| 1973 | EMI | No. not available | *Baranta One* |
| 1991 | (Solo album forthcoming) | | *Imagination* |

Francis Fuster can also be seen on the video *Graceland—The African Concert* (1987), Warner Reprise Video, WRV 38136.

Nana Ampadu

Late 1960s	PAB	001	*African Brothers Dance Band International*
1977	Afri Bros.	AB 001	*Afrohili to the USA*
1978	Justine & John	JJLP003	*Sanbra*
1982	Makossa	MA7079	*Agatha*
1982	Makossa	MA7080	*Owuo Aye Me Bi*
1983	Akonok	001	*Mentumi Ngyaa Wo*
1983	Makossa	MA7084	*Enyimba Di N'aba*
1984	Makossa	MA7087	*Nketenketenkete*
1984	Stern's	1004	*Me Poma*

1985	Afri Bros.	AB006	*Obi Doba*
1986	Afri Bros.	AB110	*Osoro Siane*
1986	Weston T.P.	WTP007	*Mebisa?*
1986	Afri Bros.	ABI1201	*Space Reggae*
1987	Afri Bros.	ABI1202	*Oman Bo Adwo*
1988	Afri Bros.	ABI1203	*Me Do Wiase*

Hedzoleh Soundz

| 1973 | Blue Thumb | BTS62 | *Masekela: Introducing Hedzoleh Soundz* |
| 1974 | Blue Thumb | BTS6015 | *Masekela: I Am Not Afraid* (Hedzoleh appears as Masekela's backing band.) |

Olatunji

1960	Columbia	CL 1412 (now PC8210)	*Drums of Passion*
1961	Columbia	CL 1634	*Zungo*
1962	Columbia	CL 1866	*Flaming Drums!*
1963	Columbia	CS 8796	*High Life!*
1964	Roulette	R25274	*Drums! Drums! Drums!*
1966	Columbia	CS 9307	*More Drums of Passion*
1986	Blue Heron	BLU706-1	*Dance to the Beat of My Drum*
1986	Rykodisc	10102	*Drums of Passion: The Invocation*
1986	Rykodisc	10107	*Drums of Passion: The Beat* (same as Blue Heron BLU706-1)

Orlando Julius Ekemode

1968	Polydor	PLP 003	*Super Afro Soul*
1985	Shanachie	43029	*Dance Afro-Beat*
1987	Melanie	JRF1015	*Sisi Shade*
1991	Ashiko	AR001	*We Pray for World Peace*

O. J. Ekemode and the Nigerian All Stars can also be seen on the *Dance Afro-Beat* video, which is sold at the band's performances.

Joni Haastrup
With Monomono:

1972	EMI	No. not available	*Give a Beggar a Chance*
1974	Capitol	ST11327	*Dawn of Awareness*
1976	Decca	No. not available	*Wake Up Your Mind* (solo album, some members of Monomono appear)

Fela Anikulapo-Kuti

This list is a selection of Fela's recordings. For a more thorough discography of the years 1970–1981, see Carlos Moore, *Fela, Fela: This Bitch of a Life*.

1970	EMI	HNLX5200	*Fela's London Scene*

With Africa 70:

1971	EMI	HNLX5090	*Open and Close*
1972	Makossa	EM2305	*Shakara*
1974	Makossa	EM2313	*Alagbon Close*
1975	Makossa	EM2315	*Expensive Shit*
1976	Creole	CRLP511	*Zombie*
1977	Kalakuta	KK001-A	*Sorrow, Tears and Blood*
1978	Phonogram	PMLP1005	*Shuffering and Shmiling*
1979	Kalakuta	KILP001	*V.I.P. Vagabonds in Power*
1979	Kalakuta	203554	*I.T.T. International Thief Thief*
1980	Kalakuta	No number	*Authority Stealing*
1981	Capitol	4N-16292	*Black President*
1981	Capitol	4N-16293	*Original Sufferhead*

With Egypt 80:

1985	Celluloid	CELL6109	*Army Arrangement* (There are two versions of this LP. Without Fela's permission, a remix was made with non-Egypt 80 personnel while he was in jail.)
1987	Mercury	833525	*Teacher Don't Teach Me Nonsense*
1989	Shanachie	43070	*Beasts of No Nation*

1990	Shanachie	43078	*Overtake Don Overtake Overtake*
1990R	Votre Dist.	760443/ 44/45	*Fela Anikulapo Kuti* vols. 1, 2, and 3 (French compilation of Fela's greatest hits)
1991R	Shanachie	44010	*Original Sufferhead* (a compilation not to be confused with Capitol 4N-16293 above)

Sonny Okosuns

1977	EMI	NEMI0232	*Papa's Land*
1977	Pathé Marconi	CO6482355	*Ozziddi For Sale*
1978	EMI	NEMI0350	*Holy Wars*
1978	Oti	OT1058	*Fire in Soweto*
1980	EMI	NEMI0530	*The Gospel of Sonny Okosuns Ozziddi*
1981	Oti	OTI0500	*Third World*
1982	Oti	OTI030	*Mother and Child*
1983	Celluloid	CEL6716	*Togetherness*
1984	His Master's Voice	HMV036	*Which Way Nigeria?*
1984R	Shanachie	43019	*Liberation* (a compilation of tracks from previous albums)
1985	His Master's Voice	HMV038	*Revolution II*
1991	Profile	PCD1414	*African Soldiers*

Compilations

	Pathé Marconi	PTX40.654	*Pont sur le Congo* (collector's item including a fine O.K. Jazz number)
	African	360.001	*L'Afrique Danse* (includes several cuts from O.K. Jazz)

Virgin	90883	*Heartbeat Soukous* (contains a nice Kanda Bongo Man track)
Rounder	11513	*Africa Moves* (one track by Nana Ampadu's African Brothers Band)
Original Music	ARM601	*Africa Dances* (both S. E. Rogie and African Jazz appear)
Original Music	OMA106	*The Tanzania Sound* (Remmy Ongala isn't here, but his roots are)
Original Music	OMA102	*The Sound of Kinshasa* (nice tracks by O.K. Jazz, African Jazz, and African Fiesta)

Bibliography

Achebe, Chinua. *Things Fall Apart*. New York: Astor-Honor, 1959.

Andriamirado, Sennen. "Franco, le chanteur qui dérangeait." *Afrique Magazine* (Paris), December 1989, 76–83.

Anikulapo-Kuti, Fela. "My Life in Prison." Interview conducted by Dele Olojede, *Newswatch* (Lagos), 12 May 1986, 12–20.

Bame, Kwabena N. *Come to Laugh*. New York: Lillian Barber Press, 1985.

Bemba, Sylvain. *50 ans de musique du Congo-Zaire*. Paris: Présence Africaine, 1984.

Bender, Wolfgang. "Ebenezer Calender—An Appraisal." In *Bayreuth African Studies Series 9: Perspectives on African Music*, ed. Wolfgang Bender, 43–68. Bayreuth: Bayreuth University, 1989.

———. *Sweet Mother*. Chicago: University of Chicago Press, 1991.

"Celebrating Culture." *West Africa* 3776 (25 December 1989): 2135.

Chernoff, John Miller. "Africa Come Back: The Popular Music of West Africa." In *Repercussions: A Celebration of African-American Music*, ed. Geoffrey Haydon and Dennis Marks, 152–78. London: Century Publishing, 1985.

Clarke, Donald, ed. *The Penguin Encyclopedia of Popular Music*. New York: Viking Penguin, 1989.

Collins, John. *African Pop Roots: The Inside Rhythms of Africa*. London: W. Foulsham & Company, 1985.

———. *Musicmakers of West Africa*. Washington: Three Continents Press, 1985.

———. *E. T. Mensah: King of Highlife*. London: Off The Record Press, 1986.

Conrath, Philippe. "Franco, la rumba à mort." *Libération* (Paris), 16 October 1989, 46.

Coplan, David. "Go to My Town, Cape Coast! The Social History of Ghanaian Highlife." In *Eight Urban Musical Cultures: Tradition and Change*, ed. Bruno Nettl, 96–114. Urbana: University of Illinois Press, 1978.

Coxson, Sarah. "The Song of Sooliman." *Folk Roots* 59 (May 1988): 17–19.

Du Bois, Victor D. "Zaire under President Sese Seko Mobutu, Part 1: The Return to Authenticity." *AUFS Fieldstaff Reports*, Central and Southern Africa Series, vol. 27, no. 1. Hanover: American Universities Field Staff, 1973.

147

Ekwensi, Cyprian. "Nana-Jagua Nana." *West African Review,* August 1957, 791.

Ewens, Graeme. *Luambo Franco and 30 Years of O.K. Jazz.* London: Off The Record Press, 1986.

Flippo, Chet. *Yesterday: The Unauthorized Biography of Paul McCartney.* New York: Doubleday, 1988.

Franco and his T.P.O.K. Jazz in U.S.A. Program for U.S. tour November–December 1983.

"Franco: Last Days in London." *Tradewind: Stern's Music Review* (London) 2, no. 11 (November 1989): 3.

George, Susan. *A Fate Worse than Debt.* New York: Grove Press, 1988.

Graebner, Werner. "Whose Music? The Songs of Remmy Ongala and Orchestra Super Matimila." *Popular Music* 8, no. 3 (October 1989): 243–58.

Graham, Ronnie. *The Da Capo Guide to Contemporary African Music.* New York: Da Capo Press, 1988.

Idowu, Lanre, with Soji Omotunde and Taiwo Obe. "The Kutis: What A Family." *This Week* (Lagos), 8 September 1986, 14–19.

Johnson, Rotimi. "The Language and Content of Nigerian Popular Music." In *Bayreuth African Studies Series 9: Perspectives on African Music,* ed. Wolfgang Bender, 91–102. Bayreuth: Bayreuth University, 1989.

Kpatindé, Francis. "La rumba s'est arrêtée." *Jeune Afrique* (Paris) 1504 (30 October 1989): 24.

Kazadi, Pierre. "Congo Music: Africa's Favorite Beat." *Africa Report,* April 1971, 25–27.

Lang, Iain. "Jazz Comes Home to Africa." *West African Review,* December 1956, 1088–90. Reprinted from *Sunday Times* (London), 16 and 23 September 1956.

Lonoh, Michel (Malangi). *Essai de commentaire sur la musique Congolaise moderne.* Kinshasa: St. Paul, 1969.

McKay, Albert. "High-Life Boom Hits West Africa." *West African Review,* January 1957, 77–78.

Mahoney, Richard D. *JFK: Ordeal in Africa.* New York: Oxford University Press, 1983.

Marck, James. "Kanda's Zaire Soukous Sound." *NOW* (Toronto), 11–17 May 1989, 23.

Moore, Carlos. *Fela, Fela: This Bitch of a Life.* London: Allison & Busby, 1982.

Nellhaus, Arlynn. "Masekela High on New Sound." *Denver Post,* 30 January 1974, 39.

"Night Out in Lagos." *West African Review,* June 1959, 482–83.

Pareles, Jon. "The Pop Life." *New York Times,* 30 November 1983, C26.

Pearson, Barry Lee. *Sounds So Good to Me*. Philadelphia: University of Pennsylvania Press, 1984.

Prince, Rob. "Le grand maitre." *Folk Roots* 79/80 (January/February 1990): 13–16.

Roberts, John Storm. *Black Music of Two Worlds*. New York: Praeger Publishers, 1972.

Rogers, S. E. *Rogie International Song Book*. Freetown, Sierra Leone: S. E. Rogers, 1970.

Stapleton, Chris, and Chris May. *African All-Stars*. London: Quartet Books, 1987.

Steffens, Roger. "Free at Last." Interview with Fela Anikulapo-Kuti, *Option*, September/October 1986, 26–29.

Stewart, Gary. "African Music Gallery." *West Africa* 3564 (16 December 1985): 2639.

———. "Out of Africa and Into America." *San Francisco Examiner/Chronicle*, Datebook Section, 15 March 1987, 39. Distributed by the Los Angeles Times Syndicate, 1987.

———. "The Silent Sage." *West Africa* 3770 (20 November 1989): 1926–27.

———. "Soukous: Birth of the Beat." *The Beat* 8, no. 6 (1989): 18–21.

———. "The Session Men." *The Beat* 8, no. 6 (1989): 28–29.

Thomas, J. C. *Chasin' the Trane*. New York: Doubleday, 1975. Reprint, New York: Da Capo Press, n.d.

Wallis, Roger, and Krister Malm. *Big Sounds from Small Peoples*. London: Constable, 1984.

Ware, Naomi. "Popular Music and African Identity in Freetown, Sierra Leone." In *Eight Urban Musical Cultures: Tradition and Change*, ed. Bruno Nettl, 296–320. Urbana: University of Illinois Press, 1978.

———. "Popular Musicians in Freetown." In *African Urban Notes* 5, no. 4 (Winter 1970): 11–18. (The author is sometimes listed as Naomi Ware Hooker.)

Waterman, Christopher Alan. *Juju: A Social History and Ethnography of an African Popular Music*. Chicago: University of Chicago Press, 1990.

Wilmer, Valerie. "Ginger Baker: Anglo Afro?" *Down Beat*, 19 March 1970, 16–17.

———. "S. E. Rogers' Life Story." In *Rogie International Songbook*, compiled by S. E. Rogers, 3–15. Freetown, Sierra Leone: S. E. Rogers, 1970.

Index

151